BIG
FLAVOURS
FROM A
SMALL
KITCHEN

CHRISKITCH

BIG FLAVOURS FROM A SMALL KITCHEN

Chris Honor &
Laura Washburn Hutton

Photography by Tamin Jones

MITCHELL BEAZLEY

An Hachette UK Company
www.hachette.co.uk

First published in Great Britain
in 2015 by Mitchell Beazley,
a division of Octopus Publishing
Group Ltd
Endeavour House
189 Shaftesbury Avenue
London WC2H 8JY
www.octopusbooks.co.uk

ISBN 978 1 84533 992 0

A CIP catalogue record for this book
is available from the British Library.

Printed and bound in China

10 9 8 7 6 5 4 3 2 1

Publisher Alison Starling
Managing Editor Sybella Stephens
Senior Art Editor Juliette Norsworthy
Photographer Tamin Jones
Designer Miranda Harvey
Food Stylist Chris Honor
Prop Stylist Liz Belton
Senior Production Manager
    Katherine Hockley

CONTENTS

INTRODUCTION

It was not a good time to open a café. It was not the best spot for one either.

It was February 2013 and the place was a small, run-down unit on a residential street in Muswell Hill, north London. It would be fair to say we were not making it easy on ourselves, but there were not many options. It was affordable and manageable for a chef on his own. Besides, I just had this feeling …

I am Christian Honor, the owner and chef of Chriskitch, a little eatery sandwiched between a secondary school and a few houses, on the site of a former chocolate factory.

These days, Chriskitch is always buzzing and, when the weather is good, there is often a lunchtime queue out front. There are now up to six members of staff at peak times, but 'little' is still the operative word. There are about eighteen covers indoors and we are open only during the day. Coffee, teas and cakes are served all day; at lunchtime we add three salads, a few breads, one main and one soup. On weekends, we do brunch. I suppose you could call it a coffee shop-trattoria, because there is no menu. What you see on the table at the front is what you get, and this changes daily.

Small is big

Watching our popularity grow so fast has been such a great feeling, not least because it shows that this is the right place at the right time. After years of working in restaurant kitchens the world over – Australia, Southeast Asia, the Middle East – opening Chriskitch was my dream. It is the culmination of all my travels and all my experience: I have seen the world, worked in some amazing places and worked my way up to running a big kitchen. Now all I want is my own little place, close to home.

Maybe this is some sort of mid-life crisis in reverse, but after years in this business I no longer want to work while everyone else plays. Because that is the reality of life as a chef. It is essentially a dysfunctional profession; it is unsociable, it is physically demanding, it is long hours for low pay, it demands allegiance to the kitchen, which means neglect of your nearest and dearest. All too high a price to pay for my liking. But I remain a chef, by vocation and by passion, and therein lies the beauty of Chriskitch. It allows me to reconcile the desire I have to cook for a living and still be part of my own life. It is a restaurant on my terms, not on restaurant terms.

What I love is knowing that doing it my way means my family is in my kitchen. My wife Bibi pretty much runs the business side and she cooks as well. Her Polish heritage has been a big influence, and you will get a lot of Eastern European flavours in Chriskitch food. The kids, Kayah and Olena, are there most days after school, like so many of the other neighbourhood kids.

Freshly cooked, every day

Understanding how the place came to be is crucial to understanding my cooking. What I cook is real food, but I'm not talking about some foodie cult of the authentic. I buy raw ingredients and I cook them. Nothing could be more basic than that. They do not go through multiple hands to get to the plate. Chriskitch is a small place and it is small-scale cooking.

My inspiration for menus comes from what I find, and I particularly like the underdog; misshapen veg and bruised fruit cost a bit less and they are still completely legitimate ingredients. I shop in pretty much the same places my customers shop in: the local supermarkets and greengrocers.

Nothing I prepare is technically complicated – I do not have that luxury, either of time or of equipment. I started with one hotplate and one oven, and that is still pretty much the entire story. If I want to get any sleep I need to keep it simple, because the food must be cooked and ready by 10 a.m. every day and I do not want to get up much before 5 a.m.

The recipes for Chriskitch evolved out of a necessity to offer flavourful food within a limited kitchen, with minimal staffing (just me in the beginning). What this means is that what I do in the kitchen can be done by anyone.

Striking a balance

Regardless of space and time, to make good food a cook needs to understand the importance of balance for both the palate and the eye. I am always thinking about the five main taste sensations: sweet, salty, spicy, sour, bitter. At the same time, I consider texture – crunchy, smooth, tender – and then there is colour and presentation. The beauty of this approach is that if you get it all right, if all the tastes and textures and visual appeal come together, you just need to mound it on a platter and it will be fantastic. My own flourish is to juxtapose unexpected flavours. It is all well and good to keep things equally balanced, but I like to throw in a few surprises. And that's all there is to it.

What I am hoping to impart by sharing my recipes is an ability to create tasty, exciting, beautiful food. In a way, this is as much guidebook as cookery book, because I do not necessarily think in terms of recipes; I think in terms of combinations. Mix up the flavours and textures and, at the same time, make it appeal to the eye. Be generous but, mostly, add a good pinch of the unanticipated. This is what I do, and this book will help you to do the same thing in your kitchen.

When Chriskitch started, it was not obvious that it would work. I knew what I wanted, but there was no master plan, my heart simply said this was the time and the place. I am a simple guy and Chriskitch is a simple idea: cook well and they will come. It is not the biggest café in Muswell Hill, but it is the best. If you don't believe me, ask one of my customers.

Chris,
London, 2015

SALADS 1

RAW SALADS

BLOOD ORANGE
FENNEL
DILL
FETA
ALMOND

SERVES 4-6

2 blood oranges
1 large fennel bulb, with fronds, thinly sliced
   with a mandoline
40g fresh dill, roughly chopped
1 tablespoon nigella seeds or whole dill seeds
60g feta cheese, crumbled
60g whole almonds, roasted
a good handful of mustard cress
a pinch of freshly ground star anise (see *Note* below)
salt and coarsely ground black pepper to taste
extra virgin olive oil, for drizzling

There is only one way to get paper-thin slices of fennel and that is with a mandoline slicer – most good kitchen shops and online suppliers offer this very simple tool that is perfect for home cooks, so there is no excuse not to have one. The skinniness does more than improve the look; with fennel it also enhances the taste. There is something superbly delicate about see-through shreds of fennel that is completely different from when it's chopped.

Trim away the top and bottom of the orange. Slice off the skin, including the white pith, and discard. Gently separate the orange segments from the membrane.

Combine all the ingredients except the oil in a big bowl. Mix with your hands, massaging gently, then mound on a platter. Drizzle with extra virgin olive oil and serve at room temperature.

Note: For star anise powder, place a small handful of whole star anise in a spice grinder and pulverise until it becomes a smooth powder. Keep in a sealed container in a dark place.

WATERMELON
FETA
PUMPKIN SEED
BASIL

The inspiration for this came from my time in the Middle East: when it is 37°C, you need a chilled watermelon salad, so think cool crisp melon and shisha tea, and let the contrasting flavours and textures transport you. Serve on a hot day, in the shade, preferably.

SERVES 8

1kg watermelon, quartered, sliced and deseeded
1 sachet of berry tea, removed from the sachet
100g feta cheese, crumbled
3 tablespoons pumpkin seeds, dry roasted
10 sprigs of fresh mint, leaves stripped and torn
10 sprigs of fresh basil, leaves stripped and torn
3 green tomatoes, halved
a handful of baby tomatoes
30ml pumpkin seed oil
2 tablespoons Basil Sugar (see page 217)

Line up the watermelon slices on a platter and sprinkle with the berry tea.

Scatter over the cheese, seeds, herbs and tomatoes. Drizzle with the oil, sprinkle with the sugar and serve.

BLUE CHEESE
ROSEMARY
COX'S APPLE
WALNUT

60g blue cheese, crumbled

60ml extra virgin olive oil

a large sprig of fresh rosemary, leaves stripped
and finely chopped

20ml grape molasses

salt and coarsely ground black pepper

30ml malt vinegar

4 Cox's apples, or other tart eating apples

100g walnuts, severely roasted and roughly chopped
(see *Note* below)

a handful of fresh spinach leaves

SERVES 4

These look so fantastic and the taste combo is beautiful, but what really makes them for us is that they are so easy to serve. One apple is one portion, so while it looks fancy and complicated, this is actually simplifying our lives by making plating up easier. You can also make this recipe with pears.

In a mixing bowl, combine the blue cheese, olive oil, rosemary leaves, grape molasses, salt and pepper and mix well. Set aside.

Put the vinegar into another bowl. Working with one apple at a time, slice the whole apples about 5mm thick, and dip the slices immediately into the vinegar – this will prevent them from discolouring.

As each apple is sliced and dipped, transfer them to the bowl with the cheese mixture and toss to coat. Remove to a platter, keeping the slices of each apple in a separate pile, then continue until all the apples are sliced and coated.

To serve, reassemble the apple slices into apple-shaped stacks, adding the roasted walnuts, spinach leaves and seasoning between layers.

Note: My recipes call for severely roasted nuts and seeds which simply means dry-frying them until they are very dark and aromatic for a more pronounced taste. 'Severely' implies stopping just short of burning.

SEAWEED
APPLE
POPPY SEED
BALSAMIC

This is my take on a traditional Japanese seaweed salad. The difference here is the presence of apples and carrots and, of course, grape molasses and a few more bits, but this upholds the basic principle of vinegar tang alongside briny, chewy seaweed. It tastes so good you wouldn't know it was good for you. This is best made at the last minute to keep it all vibrant.

10g hijiki seaweed
20g wakame
40g seaweed salad
2 small red apples
2 tablespoons vegetable oil
juice of ½ a lemon
2–3 large carrots, peeled
a pinch of icing sugar
2 teaspoons nigella seeds
2 teaspoons white poppy seeds
60ml balsamic vinegar
90ml grape molasses
1 small bunch of fresh parsley, finely chopped without stems
salt and freshly ground black pepper

Put all the seaweed into a bowl and add water to cover. Leave to stand for 10 minutes, then drain and squeeze out the excess water.

Meanwhile, slice the whole apples very thinly using a mandoline. Put them into a bowl with the oil and lemon juice and toss with your hands to coat. Set aside.

Using a julienne slicer, cut the carrots into long, thin ribbons. Alternatively, slice very thinly by hand or grate. Put them into a bowl, dust lightly with icing sugar and toss.

In a large bowl, combine everything but the carrots, apples and parsley and mix well. Just before serving, add the remaining ingredients, toss lightly and taste for seasoning. Serve immediately.

AVOCADO CORIANDER CHILLI LEMON

SERVES 4-6

4 ripe avocados

1 big bunch of fresh coriander, coarsely chopped, including stems

2 fresh red chillies, deseeded and finely chopped

zest and juice of 2 lemons

1 tablespoon coriander seeds

80ml extra virgin olive oil

salt and coarsely ground black pepper

Cooking doesn't get much easier than this. Chop, chop, everything in the bowl, mix around, serve. Done and done. The avocado turns creamy when it blends with the oil and lemon, so it seems like there is a complicated dressing thing going on when, in fact, there isn't. As much a salad as a vegetable side dish, you can also serve this with simple grilled meats or seafood.

Cut the avocados in half lengthways, then into eighths. Leave the skin on, as it helps them to keep their shape.

Put them into a mixing bowl with the remaining ingredients. Mix with your hands, massaging gently to combine. Taste and adjust the seasoning, then mound on to plates and serve.

BROCCOLI
DRIED CRANBERRY
PECAN
BASIL
ORANGE

SERVES 4–6

1 large head of broccoli

120g dried cranberries

120g toasted pecans, severely roasted (see *Note* on page 17)

½ a bunch of fresh basil

zest and juice of 1 orange

50ml extra virgin olive oil

salt and coarsely ground black pepper

A super simple salad that was inspired by something my sister Kylie once made for me and a good thing too, as this is very popular with our customers. Raw, grated and lightly dressed, this is an excellent alternative to plain boiled broccoli. If you are enthusiastic about citrus, add a bit more.

Using the large holes of a cheese grater, grate the flowery head of the broccoli into a large mixing bowl. Trim the broccoli stalk and chop it roughly.

Add the remaining ingredients and mix with your hands, massaging gently to combine. Taste and adjust the seasoning, then mound on a platter and serve.

SALMON
PINEAPPLE
FENNEL
RED ONION
DILL

500g very fresh boneless skinless salmon

1 small pineapple, about 1kg, peeled, cored and quartered

1 large fennel bulb, with fronds

1 large spring onion, sliced

1 red onion, thinly sliced

1 tablespoon dill seeds

a pinch of nigella seeds

a few sprigs of fresh dill, roughly torn

1 teaspoon pink peppercorns in brine, drained

thin strips of zest and juice of 2 lemons

30ml extra virgin olive oil

SERVES 4

A fatty fish like salmon goes well with acidic ingredients, and here caramelized pineapple bolsters the lemon tang. This is gorgeous on its own as a starter or as part of a selection for a main dish. Pair it with Avocado, Coriander, Chilli, Lemon (see page 20) and Buckwheat, Mixed Seeds, Spinach (see page 26).

With a sharp knife, cut the salmon into paper-thin slices on an angle. Set aside.

Cut the pineapple pieces in half lengthways, then slice thinly. In a non-stick skillet, dry fry the pineapple slices until caramelized on both sides. Set aside.

Keep the fennel whole and slice it lengthways, using a mandoline. Set aside. Reserve a few fronds for garnish.

Arrange alternating slices of pineapple, fennel, spring onion, red onion and salmon on a platter, then scatter the seeds, dill, peppercorns, fennel fronds and lemon zest on top.

Drizzle with the oil and lemon juice just before serving.

BUCKWHEAT MIXED SEEDS SPINACH

Nothing but grains and seeds, and a few spinach leaves, this salad is packed full of goodness. I devised this as a way to showcase seeds, but also to serve as part of our salad selection at lunchtime. It's a real team player and complements many a salad. This shines on a buffet table.

SERVES 4–6

250g buckwheat
120g sunflower seeds
120g pumpkin seeds
80g brown linseeds
80g sesame seeds
200g fresh baby spinach leaves
2 tablespoons extra virgin olive oil,
   plus extra to serve
salt and freshly ground black pepper

Cook the buckwheat according to the packet instructions. Drain and set aside.

In a large frying pan, combine all the seeds and dry fry over medium heat, tossing/stirring until aromatic and popping. Do not crowd the pan; you may need to work in batches. Transfer the toasted seeds to a plate and leave to cool to room temperature.

In a small bowl, toss together the spinach and oil and set aside.

In a glass jar or several small jars, arrange layers of the buckwheat, seeds and spinach. Serve with extra olive oil alongside. Alternatively, in a large bowl, combine the buckwheat, toasted seeds and spinach and mix gently to combine. Season to taste and serve.

CUCUMBER
WHITE POPPY SEEDS
SPRING ONION
ORANGE

Beautiful simplicity. The key to this is last-minute assembly: cucumber flesh is very porous, so it soaks up oil easily and salt makes it watery. Otherwise there is nothing to it — this is quick to pull together, as it has only a few ingredients.

SERVES 4-6

100g white poppy seeds
2 large cucumbers, washed and dried
5 red spring onions, thinly sliced at an angle
zest and juice of 1 orange
salt, to taste
extra virgin olive oil, for drizzling

In a non-stick skillet, dry fry the poppy seeds over a medium-high heat until they begin to turn golden. Transfer them to a large mixing bowl.

Slice the cucumbers lengthways with a spaghetti mandoline blade or chop into very fine matchsticks; if they are really long, halve them first.

Put the cucumbers into the bowl with the poppy seeds. Add the remaining ingredients, apart from the oil. Mix with your hands, massaging gently to combine, then mound on a platter. Taste and adjust the seasoning. Seconds before serving, drizzle on as much or as little good-quality olive oil as you like.

FARRO CAULIFLOWER MUSTARD SEED PARMESAN

SERVES 4-6

150g farro

10g black mustard seeds

10g yellow mustard seeds

2 tablespoons vegetable oil

20g wholegrain Dijon mustard

30g sunflower seeds

1 large cauliflower

40ml extra virgin olive oil

zest and juice of 2 lemons

¼ teaspoon ground turmeric

a few nasturtium leaves and garlic chive flowers (optional)

salt and freshly ground black pepper

3 hard-boiled eggs, peeled and sliced

60g Parmesan cheese, shaved

OK, I confess, keeping the cauliflower raw is all part of my time-efficient ethos. But truly, cauliflower tastes so good as it is and makes such a fantastic salad ingredient, why bother with cooking when you don't have to? Because this is basically an all-white dish, I like to add a bit of green for visual contrast. In season, nasturtium and chive flowers are wonderful and, when I can find some, a few fresh curry leaves, otherwise parsley is perfectly fine.

Cook the farro according to the packet instructions and set aside to cool.

Put all the mustard seeds into a small frying pan with 1 tablespoon of the oil and fry over a medium-high heat until they pop. Stir in the Dijon mustard to stop the cooking, then scrape the contents of the pan into a large mixing bowl.

Put the sunflower seeds into the same frying pan with the remaining tablespoon of oil and fry over a medium-high heat until they pop. Transfer to the bowl of mustard seeds.

Quarter the cauliflower, then slice thickly with a mandoline. Alternatively, use a grater. Add to the bowl of seeds.

Add the olive oil, lemon zest and juice, turmeric and the leaves and flowers, if using. Season lightly, then mix with your hands, massaging gently to combine. Taste and adjust the seasoning, then mound on a platter.

Scatter the eggs and Parmesan over the cauliflower and serve.

COOKED
SALADS

SERVES 4-6

A very green salad of beans
punctuated with a subtle hit
of chilli and chamomile. It is
important to use only a pinch of
the latter, as chamomile is quite
strong, despite appearances, and
its flavour develops over time.
It can pervade everything, so use
sparingly. Exceptionally, this
salad contains no acidic element
in the form of lemon juice or
vinegar. I find it makes the green
beans turn an unappealing shade
of green-grey, so I leave it out,
which does not affect the taste
in the slightest. This is one of
our most popular salads.

GREEN BEANS
MINT
LEMON
CHAMOMILE
DILL SEED

100g fine green French beans
salt and freshly ground black pepper
100g sugar snap peas
100g runner beans, topped and cut into lozenges
50g frozen green baby peas, defrosted
50g frozen soya beans, defrosted
1 bunch of fresh mint, finely chopped
zest of 2 lemons
a pinch of chamomile tea
2 pinches of dill seeds
2 pinches of coriander seeds
50ml extra virgin olive oil
½ a fresh red chilli, deseeded and thinly sliced

Bring a large pan of water to the boil. Add some salt, then
the French beans, sugar snaps and runner beans.

Blanch for 30 seconds, then drain immediately and either
transfer to a bowl of iced water or drain in a sieve and place
under cold running water for 1–2 minutes. Drain well.

Put all the peas and beans into a large bowl. Add the mint,
lemon zest, chamomile tea, dill seeds, coriander seeds,
oil, chilli, salt and pepper. Toss well. Taste and adjust the
seasoning, then transfer to a platter to serve.

Note: When available, we also make this salad with stink
beans, sourced from Chinese greengrocers.

ENDIVE
APPLE
POMEGRANATE
WALNUT
GOAT'S CHEESE

SERVES 4

My first encounter with this Spanish taste combo was at a tapas bar in Jerusalem. It was a bad day, that day, but the mood lifted the minute this dish arrived and it has been a favourite ever since. The quality of olive oil is always important, because inferior oil will ruin the taste of any dish, but here it is especially vital, so use cold-pressed extra virgin for the dressing. I have tinkered with the original salad, which had blue cheese, as I like the gentle creaminess of the goat's cheese; use whichever you prefer.

4 large endives, quartered
a pinch of sugar
salt, to taste
2 tablespoons vegetable oil
juice of 1 lemon
1 red apple, such as Gala
seeds from 1 small pomegranate
60g walnuts, severely roasted (see *Note* on page 17)
100g soft goat's cheese, in rough pieces
30ml cold-pressed extra virgin olive oil
a pinch of ground ginger
1 teaspoon chia seeds
a pinch of sumac, to finish
a few sprigs of fresh parsley

Put the endive quarters into a large non-stick pan. Add a pinch of sugar and salt, and drizzle very lightly with oil. Cook over a medium-high heat until golden brown, then take off the heat and leave in the pan while you do the rest.

Put the lemon juice into a large mixing bowl. Using a mandoline, carefully slice the apple thinly, whole, over the bowl so that the slices fall into the lemon juice immediately. This will prevent them from discolouring.

Add the remaining ingredients, apart from the sumac and parsley, to the apples. Mix with your hands, massaging gently to combine, then arrange on a platter or plate. Add a splodge of sumac and a few parsley sprigs and serve.

POTATO
CAPERS
DILL PICKLES
MUSTARD
CHAMOMILE

SERVES 4

Contrary to appearances, this is not a potato salad. It's an everything else salad: mustard seeds, mustard, pickles, capers, onion, lemon and shed loads of herbs. Potatoes are just an accessory, a bit player, a creamy velvety vehicle for all this flavour. To help this along, make sure you dress it while the potatoes are still warm so that they really soak everything up. Have fun here, be generous with the ingredients and chop everything coarsely – this is the opposite of refined.

500g new potatoes, scrubbed
1 teaspoon yellow mustard seeds
1 teaspoon black mustard seeds
1 small red onion, cut into thin half-moon slices
20g capers in brine
80g dill pickles, coarsely chopped
1 bunch of fresh dill, coarsely chopped
1 bunch of fresh chives, finely chopped
a good pinch of nigella seeds
zest and juice of 1 lemon
20ml extra virgin olive oil
a whopping dollop of wholegrain Dijon mustard
a pinch of chamomile tea, flower buds only
salt and coarsely ground black pepper
a splash of malt vinegar, if needed

Put the potatoes into a large pan and add cold water to cover. Bring to the boil and cook for 10–20 minutes, or until just tender when pierced with a knife. Drain.

Meanwhile, heat a non-stick pan until hot. Add all the mustard seeds and dry roast over a high heat until smoking. Remove from the heat and keep shaking the pan until the popping has stopped. Transfer to a large mixing bowl.

When the potatoes are cooked, roughly chop them and put them into the bowl while still warm. Add the remaining ingredients and mix well with your hands, massaging gently to combine. Taste and adjust the seasoning for salt, pepper and vinegar, then mound on to plates and serve.

BEETROOT
ORANGE
FETA
TARRAGON
CHILLI

2 oranges
600g cooked beetroot, peeled and quartered
125g feta cheese, crumbled
1 small bunch of fresh tarragon, leaves stripped and roughly torn
½ a fresh red chilli, deseeded and thinly sliced
balsamic or malt vinegar, for drizzling
extra virgin olive oil, for drizzling
salt and freshly ground black pepper

SERVES 4

Sweet, tart and salty, with a hit of anise-zing from the tarragon. We always dress this last-minute, on the plate, because the oil needs to be last on to keep it fresh looking. Simple, but a real winner. Feel free to use vacuum-packed cooked beetroot to make it even easier.

Finely zest the oranges, set aside the zest, then slice off the pith. Cut the oranges in half, then into thin half-moon slices.

Build up the salad on the serving plate by starting with the beetroot, about one-third of it, dispersed around the plate. Do the same with one-third of the oranges, then throw some feta, tarragon and chilli around. Repeat, alternating and building up, until all the ingredients are used up.

Sprinkle the orange zest on top.

Just before serving, drizzle over some vinegar and oil, then season and serve.

An eclectic mix of cooked and raw ingredients that finds butternut squash getting into bed with apples, mint and grapes. Weird, but wonderful. Try it.

BUTTERNUT SQUASH
MINT
ROSEMARY
ALMOND

SERVES 4–6

2 butternut squash
100g red rice, cooked and cooled
100ml grape molasses
2 apples
juice of 1 lemon
1 small bunch of fresh mint
a few sprigs of fresh rosemary, leaves stripped and chopped
1 small bunch of black grapes, grapes halved
½ fresh red chilli, deseeded and thinly sliced
150g whole almonds, roasted
50g currants
100ml extra virgin olive oil
100ml Chinese black rice vinegar
salt and freshly ground black pepper

Preheat the oven to 200°C/gas mark 6 and line a baking tray with baking parchment.

To prepare the squash, cut them in half lengthways, scoop out the seeds with a spoon and cut into 1cm-thick half-moon slices. Put into a large bowl, add the cooked rice, grape molasses and toss to coat. Arrange in a single layer on the baking tray and roast until tender when pierced with a fork, 20–30 minutes.

Slice the whole apples very thinly and coat them with the lemon juice to prevent discolouring.

Put all the ingredients except a few mint sprigs into a mixing bowl and toss gently. Mound on a serving platter, season, add the remaining mint sprigs and serve.

Note: A nice variation here is to use fresh halved figs in place of the grapes.

CARROT
GINGER
ORANGE

800g carrots, scrubbed

20g fresh root ginger, peeled and thinly sliced

zest and juice of 3 oranges

1 small orange, halved and thinly sliced

50g golden linseeds

80ml extra virgin olive oil

100ml grape molasses

1 bunch of spring onions, thinly sliced into lozenge-sized pieces

1 large bunch (about 50g) of fresh coriander, roughly chopped

2 teaspoons coriander seeds

salt and freshly ground black pepper

SERVES 6–8

This wintertime salad is a cold weather staple at Chriskitch and a good example of how to achieve a balance of flavours: the sweet molasses-infused carrots are bathed in tart orange juice with a hint of ginger warmth. Crisp spring onions and linseeds add crunch, and coriander adds visual interest as well as taste. Sunshine on a platter, almost.

Preheat the oven to 200°C/gas mark 6. Line a baking tray with baking parchment.

In a large bowl, mix the carrots with the ginger, orange juice, orange slices, linseeds and oil, then arrange in a single layer on the baking tray.

Roast until just tender when pierced with a knife – about 20–30 minutes, depending on the size of the carrots.

While the carrots are still warm, toss them with the remaining ingredients (use the same bowl as before), adding all the roasting tray juices, but keep aside a handful of the chopped coriander to sprinkle on just before serving.

Taste and adjust the seasoning. Pile on a platter, sprinkle over the reserved coriander and serve.

balance

This, for me, is one of the most important concepts in the kitchen. A dish needs to be balanced, which is not always the same thing as complex. Take this salad. It looks so much more interesting than it is. Which is not to say it does not taste amazing, but it is just roasted aubergine salad. What elevates it above the ordinary is the balance of tastes and textures going on here. Let me break it down into components.

Spicy: cinnamon, chilli flakes.

Savoury: onion powder, tahini, garlic powder.

Sweet: dates, pomegranate molasses.

Sour: vinegar.

Bitter: coriander seeds.

In addition, this has different layers of texture – smooth roasted aubergine and creamy tahini, crunchy sesame and pomegranate seeds – and it is visually exciting because of the contrasting colours: purples, green, white, red. Add to that a bit of dexterity and imagination when drizzling on the dressing, and it is no longer salad, but artwork. So go on, be balanced yet playful.

AUBERGINE
DATES
TAHINI

SERVES 6

4 aubergines
½ teaspoon fine salt
120ml vegetable oil
½ teaspoon garlic powder
½ teaspoon ground cinnamon
½ teaspoon onion powder
a pinch of ground cumin
¼ teaspoon coriander seeds, roughly crushed
½ teaspoon ground pepper
a pinch of red pepper flakes (pul biber)
250ml natural yoghurt
60ml pomegranate molasses
1 tablespoon malt vinegar
8–12 dried dates, with stones
150ml tahini
1 small bunch each of fresh mint and coriander,
   leaves stripped
2–3 tablespoons sesame seeds, dry roasted

Cut the aubergines into wedges. Put them into a large bowl with the salt and about one-third of the oil. Give it all a good mix with your hands, then add another third of the oil and repeat. Add the rest of the oil and repeat again. Leave to stand for 20 minutes.

Preheat the oven to 200°C/gas mark 6 and line a baking tray with baking parchment.

Add the spices to the bowl of aubergines and mix well. Arrange the aubergines in a single layer on the baking tray and roast until tender, 20–30 minutes.

Remove from the oven and arrange the aubergines on a platter. Drizzle over the yoghurt, pomegranate molasses and vinegar, and scatter over the dates, tahini, mint, coriander and sesame seeds.

GRAINS
AND PULSES

QUINOA
RADISH
ALMOND

When I first started serving this salad
I left the almonds whole, because I
like the way this looks and I like the
integrity of the ingredients to be on
display. But this does make it harder
to eat so, to keep the customers
happy, I began coarsely chopping the
almonds. For paper-thin radish slices
use a mandoline, carefully, otherwise
slice as thinly as you can manage with
a knife.

SERVES 4-6

225g quinoa
20ml malt vinegar
30ml extra virgin olive oil
salt and freshly ground black pepper
100g radishes, thinly sliced
100g whole almonds, roasted and roughly chopped
80ml natural yoghurt

Cook the quinoa according to the packet instructions.
Drain, put into a mixing bowl, and add the vinegar,
oil, salt and pepper. Toss well to combine.

Add the radishes and almonds and toss again.
Mound on a platter and drizzle with the yoghurt.
Season again and serve.

SALADS

AVOCADO
QUINOA
BUTTER BEANS
PISTACHIO
MINT

When I use avocados in a salad I often leave the skin on, for a number of reasons. It seems to keep the flesh from discolouring, simply because less of the unpeeled avocado comes into contact with the air. The skins also help the pieces to hold their shape and, most importantly, unpeeled means less work for the chef.

SERVES 6–8

3 avocados, skins on, stoned and cut into wedges
zest and juice of 2 lemons
½ a fresh red chilli, deseeded and thinly sliced
180g red quinoa, cooked according to the packet
    instructions, cooled
1 x 400g can of butter beans, drained
125g pea shoots
100g pistachios
1 handful of fresh mint, leaves stripped and
    roughly snipped with scissors
salt and freshly ground black pepper
120ml extra virgin olive oil
125g feta cheese

In a large bowl, toss together the avocado wedges and the lemon zest and juice.

Add the remaining ingredients, except the feta, and mix all gently to combine. Add the feta in chunks and mix lightly. Taste and adjust the seasoning (this may need a lot), then mound up on a platter and serve.

PEPPERS
RED ONION
GARAM MASALA
QUINOA
CASHEW

SERVES 4-6

I like things that sort themselves into neat serving portions, like this salad. It makes it simple to plan quantities and it is easy to dish up as well. This recipe is particularly well suited to parties because everything can be made ahead of time and assembled just before the festivities begin. It works on individual plates as well as on a big platter.

2 peppers, red and yellow, halved and deseeded

2 red onions, quartered

1 tablespoon garam masala

3–4 sprigs of fresh rosemary, leaves stripped

80ml grape molasses

30ml balsamic vinegar

80ml vegetable oil, plus a little for brushing

150g quinoa, cooked according to the packet instructions, then drained

125g cottage cheese

1 small handful of fresh parsley, roughly torn

80g cashews, roasted

salt and freshly ground black pepper

Preheat the oven to 200°C/gas mark 6.

Brush the peppers and onions lightly with oil and place them on a baking tray in the oven to roast until tender and the skin is blistered – 15–20 minutes. Turn the peppers halfway through cooking.

Remove from the oven and peel off as much of the blackened skin as possible – you need not remove all of it. Hang on to the roasting juices.

Put the semi-peeled peppers, the roasting juices and the garam masala into a large mixing bowl and toss gently to combine.

For the dressing, combine the rosemary, grape molasses, vinegar and oil in a bowl and set aside.

To serve, arrange the pepper halves on plates. Spoon some of the quinoa inside each one and let a bit dribble around the plates if you like. Plop on an onion wedge and a dollop of cottage cheese. Throw some parsley and cashews at it. Drizzle some dressing over each, then season and serve warm or at room temperature.

CELERY
PECAN
GOAT'S CHEESE

It is not often you see celery taking centre stage on the plate; it is usually just an add-on, like chopped onions. But celery has great flavour and deserves to be enjoyed for what it is, so here is a recipe to get it out of the vegetable drawer and on to the table. Equally good as a room temperature side dish for grilled meats.

SERVES 4-6

1 head of celery, stalks separated and halved
pinch of dried chamomile flowers (from a tea bag)
2 bay leaves
75g unsalted butter, cut into pieces
a few sprigs of fresh thyme
coarse sea salt
50g pecans, coarsely chopped
1 apple, thinly sliced into half moons
1 orange, zested and segmented
80g soft goat's cheese, in rough pieces
a pinch of chilli flakes
extra virgin olive oil, to taste
freshly ground black pepper

Preheat the oven to 170°C/gas mark 3½.

In a shallow baking dish, combine the celery, chamomile flowers, bay leaves, butter, thyme and salt. Spread out the celery ribs as much as possible to keep the layer thin. Splash in a few spoonfuls of water, cover with aluminium foil and cook until tender, about 1 hour.

Remove from the oven. When cool, transfer to a shallow dish and add the pecans, apple, orange, goat's cheese, chilli flakes, oil and season.

SWEET POTATO
CAVOLO NERO
RED RICE
PECAN

A feast of earthy, nutty flavours and contrasting textures of chewy rice, crunchy nuts and tender sweet potatoes. I prefer to keep the skins on my sweet potatoes because I think they taste better that way.

SERVES 6-8

800g sweet potatoes, scrubbed

200g cavolo nero

vegetable oil, for brushing

salt and freshly ground black pepper

150g red rice, cooked according to the packet
   instructions and cooled

60ml extra virgin olive oil

60ml balsamic vinegar

120g pecans

a little orange zest (optional)

Preheat the oven to 200°C/gas mark 6.

Roast the sweet potatoes whole, skins on, until tender when pierced – about 20–30 minutes. Remove from the oven and let them cool, then cut them into wedges.

Arrange the cavolo nero leaves on a baking tray, brush both sides of the leaves with vegetable oil and season lightly. Roast until crispy; timings will vary, so you need to keep an eye on them. Take them out when they are dark, but don't let them burn. Set aside and leave to cool.

Put all the ingredients into a large bowl and mix gently but thoroughly. Taste and adjust the seasoning, adding more vinegar if necessary, then serve.

WILD RICE
BLACK OLIVE
GREEN GRAPE

Chewy nutty grains, sweet juicy grapes, intense roasted olives and the sweet-sour tang of preserved olives all come together in one bowl for a blast of flavour. This salad is very unexpected and very beautiful.

SERVES 6–8

300g pitted black olives

200g black wild rice

200g pearl barley

100g preserved olives (see *Note* below), pitted and
    coarsely chopped

2 celery stalks, sliced

200g green grapes, halved

a small bunch of fresh flat-leaf parsley, roughly
    chopped, plus a few whole leaves

juice of 2 lemons

zest of 1 lemon

salt and freshly ground black pepper

Preheat the oven to 90°C/gas mark as low as possible.

Spread the black olives in a single layer on a baking tray and put them into the oven to dry out for 6–8 hours, or until fully dehydrated. Put them into a spice grinder and grind to a powder.

Cook the rice and the barley according to the packet instructions, then drain and set aside.

Put all the ingredients into a large bowl and mix gently. Taste and adjust the seasoning, then serve.

Note: Preserved olives can be found in Chinese grocers, but if difficult to source they can be omitted.

PEA SHOOTS
KALE
SAMPHIRE
GOJI BERRY
LIQUORICE

This is one of those dishes you either love or hate, I will be honest. It is out there, but I am one of the lovers. It is simply amazing to get a hit of liquorice and samphire and kale all at once, not to mention all the other tastes going on. It is very important to slice the kale really, really thin for this. It is kept raw, so is quite powerful and not as tender as when cooked, so you do not want big pieces.

SERVES 4

50g pea shoots

70g kale, very thinly sliced

a handful of rocket leaves

20g samphire

3 tablespoons goji berries, soaked in cold water for
    10 minutes to soften, then drained

½ a red onion, thinly sliced

salt and freshly ground black pepper

50g black liquorice twists, coarsely chopped

3–4 tablespoons extra virgin olive oil

60g walnuts, coarsely chopped

a little orange zest

In a large mixing bowl, combine all the ingredients and toss with your hands. Taste and adjust the seasoning, then mound on a platter or plate and serve.

CAULIFLOWER
HARISSA
BUCKWHEAT
MINT
PISTACHIO

A Moorish-inspired taste combo that involves almost no skill to pull together. All you have to do is roast the cauliflower, lay it on a plate and throw everything else on top. A masterpiece of kitchen cheating, the beauty is in the haphazardness.

3 red peppers, deseeded and sliced

1 large cauliflower, cut into 2cm-thick slices

2–3 whole garlic bulbs, halved horizontally, and 6 garlic cloves, bashed

1½ tablespoons extra virgin olive oil

salt and freshly ground black pepper

125g buckwheat

100g natural yoghurt

seeds from ½ a pomegranate

a few sprigs of fresh mint, leaves stripped

75g pistachios, roasted and roughly chopped

zest and juice of 1 lemon

2 tablespoons harissa

Preheat the oven to 180°C/gas mark 4 and line a baking tray with baking parchment.

In a mixing bowl, combine the red peppers, cauliflower, garlic and oil and toss very gently to coat evenly. Arrange in a single layer on the baking tray and season. Roast until just charred and tender, about 20 minutes.

Meanwhile, cook the buckwheat according to the packet instructions. Drain and set aside until needed.

Arrange the cooked cauliflower slices on a large platter. Drizzle over the yoghurt and sprinkle the top with the pomegranate seeds, mint, pistachios and the lemon zest and juice. Add blobs of buckwheat and harissa and serve.

LENTIL
PEPPERS
GARAM MASALA
ALMOND
CHERRY

The idea here, as with most of my cooking, is to get a balance of sweet and spicy flavours alongside soft and crunchy textures. What also makes this so appealing is the weird and wonderful partnering of ethnic ingredients; it's a sort of India meets Italy on a platter and the encounter is tremendous. Chef's cheat: it's worth making the Cherry Chutney (see page 212) just for this recipe, but even I do not always have some to hand, in which case I sprinkle on dried cranberries.

400g Puy lentils

1 tablespoon vegetable oil

5 or 6 mini peppers, red and orange mixed

2 teaspoons garam masala

2 small red apples

zest and juice of 1 lemon

1 x 400g can of chickpeas, drained

80g whole almonds, severely roasted (see *Note* on page 17)
    and roughly chopped

a few sprigs of fresh basil, leaves stripped and torn

fine sea salt

180g ricotta cheese

3–4 tablespoons Cherry Chutney (see page 212)

honey, for drizzling

balsamic vinegar, to serve

Cook the lentils according to the packet instructions, then drain and set aside to cool.

Heat the oil in a non-stick pan, add the peppers and cook over a high heat until they soften. Add the garam masala, then lower the heat and continue cooking, stirring, for another minute or so. Remove from the heat.

With a mandoline, cut the apples into batons. Alternatively, slice them thinly with a knife or evenly dice. Put them into a small bowl with the lemon juice and toss gently to coat. Set aside.

In a large mixing bowl, combine the lentils, chickpeas, spiced peppers, almonds, apples, basil and a good pinch of salt and toss gently with your hands to combine.

Mound up on a platter and top with blobs of ricotta. Drizzle over the Cherry Chutney and some honey, add a few splashes of balsamic and serve.

COUSCOUS
LEEK
LEMON
PUMPKIN SEED
CHILLI

I like leeks. They are different, they taste amazing, they are easy to cook and not too expensive. Often, they are merely a component in a recipe, but here they are centre stage on a salad plate. To add a bit more substance I have teamed them with plump pearls of Israeli couscous, some seeds for crunch and taste and fresh herbs. Simple, tasty, striking.

SERVES 4

80g moghrabieh couscous
3 leeks, roots and tops trimmed
zest of 1 lemon, plus 1 tablespoon juice
salt and freshly ground black pepper
1 tablespoon pumpkin seeds, severely roasted
  (see *Note* on page 17)
1 tablespoon sunflower seeds, severely roasted
zest of ½ an orange
½ a fresh red chilli, deseeded and finely chopped
a few sprigs of fresh parsley or coriander, leaves chopped
1 tomato, deseeded and peeled, diced
extra virgin olive oil, for drizzling
mustard cress, snipped, to serve

Cook the couscous according to the packet instructions.

Put the leeks into a large pan (cut the leeks into thirds if your pan is not big enough) and add cold water to cover. Add the lemon juice and a good pinch of salt and bring to a gentle boil over a medium heat, then lower the heat and simmer until tender, about 45 minutes. Cut the leeks into 8cm lengths and drain well on kitchen paper. (If you cut the leeks into thirds before cooking, make sure they are completely dry before assembling the salad, otherwise the cooking liquid will dilute the whole thing.)

In a large bowl, combine the couscous, pumpkin seeds, sunflower seeds, lemon and orange zest, chilli, herbs, tomato and lots of pepper. Toss gently with your hands to combine. Taste and adjust the seasoning.

To assemble, stand a few leeks upright on each plate, top with the couscous, drizzle over a bit of olive oil, scatter on some cress and serve.

BRUNCH 2

EGGS

SERVES 1

Eggs are just so fantastic — you cannot have too many recipes in your repertoire. This is a Turkish variation on shakshuka, made with spinach in place of tomatoes and peppers, and it uses some amazing flavour contrasts: cumin, raisins, chilli, lemon. The key here is temperature control: the heat needs to be high enough to cook the eggs through to the top but not too high, because the eggs stay in the pan for serving and cast iron conducts heat. But this makes it sound more complicated than it really is. The spinach acts as an insulating layer, so really there is nothing to worry about. Just cook, eat, enjoy.

EGG
YOGHURT
SPINACH
CHILLI
RAISIN

1 tablespoon extra virgin olive oil
1 garlic clove, bashed and finely chopped
50g baby spinach leaves
2 tablespoons bio-live yoghurt
3 eggs
2 tablespoons raisins
¼ of a fresh red chilli, deseeded and sliced
a scattering of toasted pumpkin seeds
1 tablespoon toasted cumin seeds
salt and freshly ground black pepper
flatbreads, for serving

Heat the oil in a 20cm cast iron frying pan. Add the garlic and cook until it just goes golden around the edges.

Add all but a few leaves of the spinach and cook for a few seconds or until just wilted.

Add dollops of the yoghurt, in separate spots, over the spinach. When the yoghurt starts to bubble, crack in the eggs. Sprinkle over the raisins, chilli, pumpkin seeds and cumin seeds.

Lower the heat and cook until the egg white is cooked through. Season to taste with salt and pepper, throw on the remaining spinach and serve immediately, with flatbreads.

PARMA HAM
BREAD
EGG
WATERCRESS
MAYONNAISE

SERVES 1

2 slices of Parma ham
2 thick slices of day-old bread
15g butter
1 egg
sea salt and freshly ground black pepper
1 lettuce heart, preferably butterhead lettuce,
    leaves separated
a few sprigs of watercress
a walloping spoonful of mayonnaise
1 teaspoon Dijon mustard

In a non-stick frying pan, cook the Parma ham until really crispy. Set aside while you prepare the eggs.

Cut a circular hole in the middle of one of the bread slices, then butter both slices on one side.

Using the same non-stick pan, put the hollowed slice butter side down, then crack an egg into the hole and cook over a high heat until the white is opaque right through or cooked to your desired doneness. Flip it over to cook on the other side. Temperature control is important; use a high heat to firm up the white quickly, but don't cook too long on either side to keep the yolk runny. Season with salt and pepper.

Transfer to a plate and top with the lettuce leaves, watercress and the Parma ham. Smear mayonnaise and mustard on the other slice of bread and set on top, mayo side down. Serve immediately.

There are no rules about what time of day is best for a sandwich, or indeed which meal is most suited to eggs. This will be good no matter when it is served.

65

TOMATO
SAUSAGE
EGG
CINNAMON
CHILLI

These leak and ooze when baking, but you don't want to lose any of the drippy bits, so it's best to bake them in a container you can also serve them from, like a mini ovenproof frying pan or a porcelain ramekin.

4–6 large whole tomatoes

1 tablespoon vegetable oil

1 large red onion, roughly chopped

2 sausages, preferably Polish sausages, or cooking chorizo, finely chopped

3 garlic cloves, chopped

1 teaspoon ground cinnamon

1 fresh red chilli, deseeded and finely chopped

zest and juice of 1 lemon

1 x 400g can of white beans, drained

a few sprigs of fresh thyme

a good pinch of nigella seeds

4–6 eggs

Preheat the oven to 160°C/gas mark 3.

Slice the tops off the tomatoes and set aside, then scoop out and discard the insides.

Heat the oil in a pan, add the onion and cook until opaque.

Add all the remaining ingredients, except the eggs, and cook for a minute or so, then transfer this mixture to the hollowed-out tomatoes, dividing it equally between them. Only fill them about two-thirds of the way up or less, depending on the size of the tomatoes, so that you have enough room at the top of each one for an egg.

Break an egg into each tomato and replace the tomato tops, then arrange the filled tomatoes in mini ovenproof frying pans or heatproof dishes of some sort, and bake until the egg has set. Serve.

EGG
MAYONNAISE
RADISH
CHIVES

8 eggs, hard-boiled, peeled and halved
100g mayonnaise
100g radishes, thinly sliced
a large handful of fresh chives, plus a few chive
   flowers if available, snipped with scissors
salt and freshly ground black pepper

SERVES 4

These are the eggs my mother-in-law serves for breakfast and it is a very good way to start the day; whoever started the vicious rumour about mothers-in-law is sorely misinformed. At Chriskitch we make this with radishes, which is a slight deviation from the original Polish farmhouse version, but it looks beautiful and adds a nice peppery crunch.

Arrange the hard-boiled eggs on a serving platter and spoon blobs of mayonaise on top of the eggs. Sprinkle over the radishes and chives. Season to taste, then serve.

BEEF MINCE
CUMIN
ONION
EGG
LEMON

SERVES 4–6

1 teaspoon ground ginger

1 teaspoon ground cumin

1 teaspoon yellow mustard seeds

½ teaspoon ground turmeric

500g beef mince

1 small red onion, thinly sliced

½ a bunch of fresh parsley, leaves stripped and kept whole

½ a fresh red chilli, deseeded and pith removed,
    finely sliced

8 eggs

1 tablespoon harrisa

salt and freshly ground black pepper

juice of 1 lemon

sourdough toast, for serving

In my family we call this Eggs & Army, but no one can remember why. This is my Lebanese grandmother's recipe and it is a traditional Lebanese dish. I love it; I always have. Serve it as part of a breakfast meze, or as a light supper dish.

In a large non-stick frying pan, combine all the spices and cook, stirring, until aromatic. Add the beef mince and onion and continue, stirring, until browned and cooked through. Stir in the parsley and chilli.

Crack in the eggs, one at a time. Cook over a medium-low heat, stirring gently, until the eggs are almost set. Remove from the heat, add the harissa and continue stirring, letting the eggs finish cooking in the residual heat of the pan.

Season with salt and pepper and the lemon juice, then serve immediately, with sourdough toast.

AVOCADO
EGG
ROCKET
CHICKPEAS
FLATBREAD

SERVES 4

My local greengrocer has an
amazing array of Turkish
groceries and I have discovered
some fantastic ingredients
shopping there. This recipe uses
a very particular sort of Turkish
cheese, which comes in a jar.
It is tart and has a spreading
consistency similar to very thick
cream cheese. Cottage cheese
comes close, but it does not have
the same tang, so feta mixed
with Greek yoghurt is a better
alternative.

1 ripe avocado

zest and juice of 1 lemon

4 eggs

1 tablespoon malt vinegar

4 large flatbreads

extra virgin olive oil, for drizzling

200g hummus

about 200g Turkish skimmed milk cheese

coarse sea salt and freshly ground black pepper

12 sun-dried tomatoes

1 spring onion, sliced

about 30g fresh rocket

1 x 400g can of chickpeas, drained

80g feta cheese

about 20g pitted black olives

pumpkin seed oil (optional)

Halve, stone and thinly slice the avocado, leaving
the skin on. Put into a bowl with the lemon juice
and some of the zest and toss to coat. Set aside.

Bring some water to the boil. Add the vinegar, then
lower the heat and poach the eggs, one at a time for
just a few minutes. Set aside on a plate.

Heat the oven to 180°C/gas mark 4. Put the flatbreads
into the oven for just a few minutes, to warm and
crisp slightly, then remove.

For each flatbread assemble as follows: drizzle with
olive oil, then smear a big splodge of hummus in
the middle. Top this with a splodge of the cheese.
Sprinkle over some salt. Put 3 sun-dried tomatoes
on each.

Add the spring onion and rocket to the bowl of
avocado and toss to mix, then divide this between
the flatbreads. Sprinkle over some chickpeas,
the feta and a few olives. Top each bread with
a poached egg and a bit more cheese, then drizzle
with a bit more olive oil, or pumpkin seed oil if you
have it, then serve.

BEEF MINCE
MUSHROOM
BACON
EGG
BAKED BEANS

SERVES 4

A breakfast burger, why not? This is pretty much a Full English but with a more playful presentation. For a vegetarian version, substitute hash brown slices for the beef. This is really fun to make and even more amusing to eat. Enjoy!

400g beef mince
100g black pudding
salt and freshly ground black pepper
Worcestershire sauce
1–2 tablespoons vegetable oil
4 portobello mushrooms
4 rashers of bacon
4 eggs
1 x 400g can of baked beans
brown sauce, to serve
4 burger buns
unsalted butter, at room temperature
a handful of fresh rocket leaves
1–2 large tomatoes, enough for 4 thick slices

Put the mince into a small bowl. Remove the casing from the black pudding and crumble in. Add a pinch of salt and pepper and a little Worcestershire sauce and mix well. Form into patties and set aside.

In a non-stick pan, heat the oil. Add the mushrooms and cook until soft, 3–4 minutes per side. Season lightly, then remove from the pan and set aside.

Using the same pan, fry the bacon until crispy on both sides and set aside. Add a bit more oil to the pan if needed and fry the eggs one at a time, 2–3 minutes, according to personal preference, transferring each one to a plate.

Using the same non-stick pan, cook your beef patties for 4–5 minutes each side over a medium-high heat. About 1–2 minutes before the patties are done, add the beans to the pan to get them warm.

Meanwhile, halve and butter the buns.

To assemble each burger, set the bottom half of a bun on a plate and top with some rocket, a patty, some brown sauce, then the tomato, mushroom, bacon and egg. Pour some beans over and top with the other bun half. Serve with more sauce on the side.

MEZE

PEPPERS
SALMON
DILL
VODKA

SERVES 4

A summery dish of lightly sugar-salt and vodka cured salmon that brings together star anise, dill and mandarin for an unexpected but completely delightful encounter. It also looks great without much effort. Fantastic flavour with minimal fuss – what more could you want?

4 long thin red peppers, kept whole
1 tablespoon vegetable oil
500g very fresh boneless skinless salmon,
   cut into 1cm cubes
1 tablespoon extra virgin olive oil, to serve
a large handful of fresh dill, roughly chopped,
   to serve
a pinch of chilli flakes
zest of ½ a lemon

FOR THE MARINADE
a pinch each of salt and sugar
1 teaspoon nigella seeds
1 teaspoon fennel seeds
a pinch of ground star anise (see page 13)
1 teaspoon Dijon mustard
1 teaspoon ground dried mandarin peel
  (see *Note* below)
2 fresh mandarins, peeled and segmented
1 small red onion, finely sliced
30ml vodka
juice of ½ a lemon

Preheat the oven to 180°C/gas mark 4.

Brush the peppers lightly with the oil, then arrange in a single layer on a baking tray. Roast until tender – about 10–15 minutes – turning halfway through cooking. Remove and leave to cool.

Meanwhile, combine all the marinade ingredients in a shallow glass or ceramic dish. Add the salmon cubes and toss well to coat. Cover, then refrigerate for about 20 minutes.

When the peppers are cool, make a cut lengthways through one side of the flesh, then arrange on a platter. Fill the peppers with the salmon mixture. Drizzle over the olive oil and sprinkle with the dill, chilli flakes and lemon zest. Serve.

Note: To make your own dried mandarin peel, put the pieces of peel on a plate and microwave on high, 1 minute at a time, until dehydrated. Grind to a powder in a spice grinder.

combining dishes for a meze

Lots of little plates for sharing is such a fun way to eat, and we do that often
for our weekend brunch. The Chriskitch twist is to make the array unexpected,
so alongside a few favourites I like to add some surprises. Radishes with butter
is a good one, because the crunch and bite is a fantastic way to get the palate
going, and Melon Ambrosia ticks the fresh fruit box but with a retro twist. It is
the salad my mum made when I was a kid: marshmallows and maraschinos and tinned
mandarins. Back in the day, it might have been dressed with mayonnaise, but we use
yoghurt; still creamy, but with a bit more tang and perfect for a late-morning meal.

RADISH
BUTTER
SALT

2 bunches of radishes (about 3–4 radishes per person)
about 100g good-quality unsalted butter,
    at room temperature
coarse sea salt
Flavoured Salt (see page 217)
coarsely ground black pepper
a handful of unsalted nuts and seeds, such as
    walnuts, almonds and watermelon seeds,
    coarsely chopped

Make a criss-cross slit in the bottom of each radish,
not going all the way through. Put them into a bowl of
iced water to soak for 10 minutes.

Meanwhile, whisk the butter to lighten it, beating
vigorously until it turns a pale lemon colour. Prepare
small bowls with the salt, pepper and nuts.

Remove the radishes from the water and pat dry. With
a small spoon, stuff a bit of the butter into each radish
criss-cross. Serve the radishes with the seasonings.

MELON
MINT
MARSHMALLOW
COCONUT
MANDARIN

SERVES 4–6

1 whole melon, well washed
1 small bunch of fresh mint, leaves stripped and
    roughly chopped
a good handful of marshmallows, large or small
40g desiccated coconut, toasted
40g hazelnuts, roughly chopped
1 x 300g can of mandarins, drained
1 small can of pineapple pieces, drained
125g natural yoghurt
honey, for drizzling
a few maraschino cherries, to decorate

Cut the melon into wedges, discard the seeds,
and put into a big mixing bowl. Add the mint,
marshmallows, coconut, nuts, mandarins, pineapple
and yoghurt and toss gently with your hands to blend.

Mound on a serving platter, drizzle with a little
honey and top with a few cherries. Serve.

WALNUT
LEMON
PEPPERS
CUMIN
CHILLI

This is nothing new – it's muhammara, which is a Syrian walnut-red pepper dip. It should be the new hummus. The amount here is generous, but should you have any left, it keeps well in the fridge. Just keep it in a sealed container.

SERVES 4–6

200g walnuts, roasted
juice of 3 lemons
6 red peppers, deseeded and roughly chopped
1 teaspoon cumin seeds, toasted
4 garlic cloves, peeled
1 fresh red chilli, deseeded and roughly chopped
salt and freshly ground black pepper
extra virgin olive oil, for drizzling
honey, for drizzling

In a pan, combine all the ingredients except the olive oil and honey and cook over a medium heat for 5–10 minutes until the garlic has softened.

Transfer to a food processor and blitz until smooth.

Place in a bowl, drizzle with some oil and honey and serve.

Note: You can add a tomato with all the other ingredients if you like, and a handful of chopped fresh parsley before serving, too.

SQUID
FENNEL
HONEY
FENUGREEK
FENNEL SEED

SERVES 4–6

1kg frozen whole squid tubes, defrosted
1 tablespoon vegetable oil

FOR THE MARINADE
1 medium fennel bulb, finely chopped,
    fronds reserved
60ml honey
1 small handful of fresh dill,
    finely chopped
1 tablespoon fenugreek seeds
1 teaspoon fennel seeds
1 teaspoon cumin seeds, toasted
6 garlic cloves, finely chopped
20g fresh ginger, grated or finely
    chopped
1 tablespoon dried fenugreek leaves
1 fresh green chilli, deseeded and
    finely chopped
zest and juice of 2 lemons
130ml extra virgin olive oil
salt and freshly ground black pepper

Unusually for us, this has a lot of finely chopped ingredients. The reason is that the squid marinates overnight, so we prep it at the end of the day, when there is a bit less time pressure. When we arrive in the morning, there is nothing to do but sear the squid. To really bring out the flavour of this dish, I dry fry the cumin seeds before adding them to the marinade. This recipe works well with most other seafood.

One day before serving, prepare the squid. Make a long slit to open up each tube and lay it flat. Use the edge of the knife to scrape it clean if any bits are left on. Score in a diamond pattern, making sure not to cut all the way through.

In a shallow glass or ceramic baking dish, combine all the marinade ingredients and stir. Add the squid and toss to coat evenly, then cover with cling film and leave to marinate in the fridge overnight.

Remove the squid from the fridge at least 30 minutes before cooking.

Heat the oil in a large non-stick frying pan. Take the squid out of the marinade with a slotted spoon and add to the pan. Sauté over a high heat until nicely seared all over. Discard the remaining marinade.

Mound the squid up on a plate, decorate with a few fennel fronds and serve.

SARDINE
PEPPERS
LEMON
GARLIC

A posh, but uncomplicated, version of sardines on toast, this is especially great for a very late, very lazy weekend brunch. Serve it with extra bread, and even a fried or poached egg, to keep you going until supper.

SERVES 2–4

4–8 whole sardines, skin scored (2 per person)
12 red peppers, stalks removed and deseeded
1 tablespoon vegetable oil
2–4 thick slices of Potato, Rosemary bread
  (see page 168), toasted
80g pitted black olives
a large handful of fresh parsley, leaves stripped
salt and freshly ground black pepper

FOR THE MARINADE
zest and juice of 2–3 lemons
100ml extra virgin olive oil
8–10 garlic cloves, thinly sliced
1 red onion, grated
1 teaspoon chilli flakes

Put all the marinade ingredients into a shallow glass or ceramic baking dish, reserving a small amount of lemon zest for garnish, and stir to blend. Add the sardines and toss to coat evenly, then cover with cling film and leave to marinate in the fridge for 30 minutes.

Meanwhile, make the red pepper paste. Put the peppers into a blender with 2–3 tablespoons of water and blitz until smooth. Transfer to a pan and bring to the boil, then lower the heat and simmer until reduced and syrupy. Leave to cool.

Heat the vegetable oil in a large non-stick frying pan. Take the sardines out of the marinade with a slotted spoon and add them to the pan – no need to brush off any bits of the marinade that may come with them. Pan fry the sardines for 3–5 minutes each side, then transfer to a plate and set aside.

Spread the toasted bread with the red pepper paste. Throw a few olives and some parsley leaves on top, then add 2 sardines per slice and scatter over the reserved lemon zest. Serve.

BANANA
PANCETTA
MAPLE SYRUP

In Australia, I would do these
on the barbecue, and that is how
this recipe evolved. But they
work just fine inside, in a pan,
so don't let cooking methods hold
you back. These are fantastic
whichever way you cook them.
Good things to serve these with
include fried eggs, a stack of
pancakes or French toast.

SERVES 4

4 just-ripe bananas, peeled
12–16 slices of pancetta
1 tablespoon vegetable oil
freshly ground black pepper
maple syrup, to serve

Wrap the bananas in the pancetta, leaving the
ends exposed. Sprinkle lightly with pepper.

Heat the the oil in a large non-stick frying
pan. When hot, add the bananas and cook until
well browned all over, 5–7 minutes. Serve hot,
drizzled with maple syrup.

TOMATO
CINNAMON
ORANGE
ALMOND

Tomatoes are one of those ingredients that are just as good long cooked as they are freshly picked. This recipe goes for cooking, but to a sort of intermediary stage. The tomatoes roast just enough for the heat of the oven to heighten the natural sugars, but not so long that they break down completely. Blissfully simple, to help with a gentle wake-up, this is lovely as part of a weekend brunch meze because it goes so well with so many things.

SERVES 4–6

4–6 large plum tomatoes
1 red onion, sliced into 4 rounds (or 6 if using 6 tomatoes)
25g unsalted butter, melted
4 garlic cloves, bashed
a pinch of ground cinnamon
1 teaspoon coriander seeds
juice of 1 orange
salt and freshly ground black pepper
120g Greek yoghurt
80g whole almonds, severely roasted (see *Note* on page 17) and coarsely chopped

Preheat the oven to 200°C/gas mark 6. Make horizontal slits all around each tomato, quite close together.

Put the tomatoes and the onion slices on a baking tray and brush with the melted butter. Sprinkle with the garlic, cinnamon, coriander seeds, orange juice, salt and pepper.

Bake for 15–20 minutes, or until the garlic is soft, but do not overcook or the tomatoes will become too soft.

To serve, put the roasted tomatoes and onion slices on plates alongside a dollop of yoghurt. Sprinkle over the almonds and top with the cooking juices and garlic from the baking tray. Serve lukewarm or at room temperature.

FAVA BEANS
GARLIC
TOMATO
CUMIN
LEMON

SERVES 4–6

This classic Middle Eastern bean purée (*ful medames*) is dead easy to make, but the cooking technique is key. When simmering all the ingredients, the goal is to evaporate the liquid and concentrate the flavours, so cook it down but not too quickly. Go slowly and use your cook's intuition; if it reduces before the flavours have had time to mingle properly, add a bit of water to keep it going.

1 tablespoon vegetable oil
1 small onion, finely chopped
4 garlic cloves, finely chopped
1 small potato, peeled, cooked and diced
1 large tomato, chopped
½ teaspoon chilli flakes
½ teaspoon ground cumin
½ teaspoon ground cinnamon
a pinch of ground turmeric
a pinch of ground cloves
1 x 400g can of fava beans, drained
juice of 1 lemon
a pinch of salt
honey, to taste
natural yoghurt, to serve
flatbreads, to serve

In a pan, combine the oil and onion and cook until soft. Add the garlic and potato and cook, stirring, for about 1 minute. Add the tomato and cook for 1–2 minutes more.

Add the spices and cook, stirring, until the mixture becomes aromatic.

Add the beans, lemon juice and a pinch of salt and cook over a very low heat, stirring occasionally, until the mixture begins to thicken. Add water if necessary to keep the consistency soft.

Purée in a blender or with a stick blender, then taste and adjust the seasoning.

Transfer to a bowl, drizzle with honey to taste and serve with yoghurt and flatbreads.

SHALLOT
LARDONS
BUCKWHEAT
MASCARPONE
THYME

SERVES 4-6

Because this is designed to be
served early in the day, and as
part of a multi-course meze,
I like to keep the flavours
interesting but not overly
complex. So the sweet, mellow
shallot becomes a vessel to
contain some chewy buckwheat mixed
with creamy mascarpone, salty
lardons and earthy thyme, all
glistening with lightly reduced
balsamic. A delightful dish to
gently set a weekend in motion.

6 banana shallots, peeled and root ends trimmed

6 garlic cloves, bashed

1 litre chicken stock

200g lardons, chopped

1 red pepper, deseeded and julienne sliced

1 bay leaf

3 teaspoons dried thyme

150g cracked wheat

100g buckwheat, soaked in cold water for 2–3 hours or overnight,
   then drained

80g mascarpone

15g unsalted butter

60ml balsamic vinegar

salt and freshly ground black pepper

sprigs of fresh thyme

Preheat the oven to 160°C/gas mark 3.

Arrange the shallots in a single layer on a baking
tray and roast for 15–20 minutes ,or until tender
when pierced.

Peel and finely chop 2 garlic cloves and set aside.

Put the stock, lardons, red pepper, bay leaf, dried
thyme and the chopped garlic into a pan and simmer
until reduced by three-quarters. Stir in the cracked
wheat and buckwheat. Remove from the heat, season
with salt and pepper and stir in the mascarpone. Set
aside for 30 minutes for the wheat to absorb the liquid.

Separate the roasted shallot layers carefully,
discarding the insides and leaving the outer layers
as a shell, and fill each shell with some of the
cracked wheat mixture. Set the filled shells on a
clean work surface or board as you go.

Melt the butter in a large non-stick frying pan.
Add the shallots, balsamic, the remaining garlic
cloves and thyme sprigs and cook until caramelized.

Transfer to plates, scraping out the pan juices and
bits, and serve.

CHIA SEED
HEMP MILK
YOGHURT
BLUEBERRY
WALNUT

SERVES 4

Pastries aside, brunch does not need to be a savoury-only affair. This is a lovely little fruity number that is packed full of good things. It is very easy to throw together and looks great layered up in small glasses for individual portions. Pass around extra honey so that diners can sweeten to taste.

125ml hemp milk, warmed
125ml water
2 heaped tablespoons chia seeds
1 tablespoon palm sugar
180g Greek yoghurt
1–2 tablespoons honey, plus extra for serving
1 small ripe but not overripe banana, sliced
125g blueberries
50g walnuts, roughly chopped
2 heaped tablespoons raisins
icing sugar, for dusting

In a mixing bowl, combine the milk, water and chia seeds and leave to stand for about 30 minutes to soften the seeds.

Mix together the sugar, yoghurt and honey. Set aside.

To assemble, divide the chia mixture between two bowls. Divide the first bowl of chia seeds evenly between your four glasses, top each with half the banana slices, half the blueberries, half the walnuts and half the raisins, then spoon one-quarter of the yoghurt into each glass. Repeat the chia and banana layers, then top with a mixture of the remaining blueberry, nut and raisins.

Drizzle with honey, sprinkle with icing sugar and serve.

SOUPS 3

POTATO
EGG
CURED HAM
PARMESAN
GARLIC

A classic combination of
ingredients - potatoes, eggs and
ham - brought together here in
a soup, for something out of the
ordinary. It is also a fantastic
way to recycle Parmesan rinds,
which have so much flavour but so
often go to waste. If you have
a milk frother, put a bit on the
top for serving.

50g butter

1 onion, diced

1 garlic clove, finely chopped

4 baked potatoes, skins on, roughly chopped

1 piece of Parmesan cheese rind, whatever size you have

1.5 litres chicken or vegetable stock

salt and freshly ground black pepper

4 slices of cured ham, such as Parma

2 tablespoons vinegar (any)

4 eggs

frothed milk, to serve (optional), or use a dollop of
  soured cream

freshly ground black pepper

In a large pan, combine the butter, onion and
garlic over a medium heat and cook until soft
and golden brown.

Add the potatoes, Parmesan rind and stock and
bring to the boil. Season lightly, then lower the
heat and simmer for 45 minutes.

Remove the rind and purée the soup. Taste and
adjust the seasoning.

In a large non-stick pan, fry the Parma ham slices
until crispy. Set aside to drain on kitchen paper.

Just before serving, make sure the soup is piping
hot. Fill a shallow pan with water, about 3cm deep,
and add the vinegar. Bring to the boil, then lower
the heat to medium.

Fill the soup bowls with hot soup and set to one side.

Gently crack the eggs into the simmering water and
poach for just a few minutes. Using a slotted spoon,
transfer one egg to each of the soup bowls. Top each
egg with a slice of fried ham and a dollop of milk
froth, and season with black pepper.
Serve immediately.

POTATO
MUSHROOM
CARAWAY SEED

SERVES 4–6

I am very fortunate to have some fabulous people working with me. This recipe comes from my assistant Voi, who grew up in Prague and is a great chef. His style of cooking fits in well with the Eastern European vibe we have going at Chriskitch: solid, hearty fare for folks who do not have time to fuss about in the kitchen. This is easily a meal in itself.

500g potatoes, peeled and diced
1.2 litres cold water
175g dried mushrooms
½ teaspoon caraway seeds
250ml milk
250ml double cream
80g plain flour
salt and freshly ground black pepper
a small bunch of fresh chives, chopped
3–4 tablespoons malt vinegar
4 hard-boiled eggs

Put the potatoes into a pan with the cold water. Bring to the boil, then lower the heat and simmer until they are just tender.

Add the mushrooms and caraway seeds and cook for a further 15 minutes.

Meanwhile, in a separate bowl, whisk together the milk, cream and flour. If there are any lumps remaining, pass the mixture through a sieve. Add a ladleful of the hot soup and whisk it into the cream mixture to blend, then pour this back into the main pan, stirring all the while.

Simmer for a further 5 minutes, then taste and adjust the seasoning. Remove from the heat and stir in the chives and vinegar.

To serve, peel and squish the eggs. Ladle the soup into bowls, top with egg bits and serve.

CARROT
GINGER
COCONUT
CHILLI

My wife and I had this,
or something similar, when
travelling through Thailand.
It is very basic, but the
combination stuck in my memory
because it was such a relief to
eat food that was simple yet
still very much about the place
we were in. We had been on the
road for a while at this point,
and tasting everything, which
is great, but also overwhelming.
This soup, served chilled, was
a refreshing respite from the
flavour assault.

60g butter
600g carrots, peeled and chopped
1 onion, finely chopped
1 large potato, peeled and chopped
25g piece of fresh ginger, peeled and finely chopped
1.5 litres vegetable or chicken stock
375ml coconut cream
salt and freshly ground black pepper
a pinch of chilli flakes
80g roasted peanuts, chopped

Melt the butter in a large pan, then add the carrots, onion, potato and ginger and cook until just soft, about 10 minutes.

Add the stock, coconut cream, salt and pepper. Bring to the boil over a medium-high heat, then lower the heat and simmer for 20–30 minutes until the vegetables are cooked through and tender.

Remove from the heat and allow to cool slightly, then purée in batches in a blender until smooth. Taste and adjust the seasoning.

To serve, ladle into bowls and top with the chilli flakes and roasted peanuts. Serve hot or cold.

CHICKEN
VERMICELLI
PARSLEY
PUMPKIN SEED OIL

How do you liven up a classic? By playing around with presentation – really, this is just a simple chicken soup. Because the chicken is poached in chicken stock, the resulting broth has a lovely concentrated flavour that serves as a background to the intensity of the pumpkin seed oil. The overall effect is elegant and striking, so this is a good one for entertaining. You may need to get a butcher to trim the chicken legs for you.

SERVES 4–6

40ml vegetable oil

2 onions, finely chopped

2 celery stalks, finely chopped

4 garlic cloves

4–6 chicken drumsticks, trimmed

1.2 litres chicken stock

salt and freshly ground black pepper

a few tablespoons of pumpkin seeds

100g vermicelli

80g unsalted butter

a few leaves of fresh parsley

80ml pumpkin seed oil

In a large pot, combine 2 tablespoons of the oil with the onion, celery and garlic and cook over a gentle heat, stirring occasionally, until just soft. Do not over-brown the vegetables.

Add the chicken drumsticks, the stock, season, then simmer over a low heat, uncovered, for 1–1½ hours.

Meanwhile, dry fry the pumpkin seeds in a non-stick pan. As soon as they start popping, remove from the heat.

Bash up the vermicelli a bit, by crushing them with the end of a rolling pin.

In another non-stick frying pan, combine the remaining vegetable oil, the butter and the vermicelli and fry until deep golden. Remove from the pan.

Ladle the broth into your bowls and add a few parsley leaves. Put a chicken leg into each bowl, bone sticking up. Place a good pinch of fried vermicelli on the end of each bone and top with a parsley leaf. Drizzle pumpkin seed oil around, scatter over some pumpkin seeds and serve.

PEPPERS
TOMATO
BASIL
OLIVE OIL

This may look unassuming, but the taste is astonishing – pure essence of red pepper sweetness. It is so beautiful on its own that, unusually for me, I have left it relatively unadorned and simple – just basic Mediterranean flavours, to be enjoyed for what they are.

SERVES 4–6

60ml extra virgin olive oil

2 tablespoons vegetable oil

1 onion, chopped

1 fresh red chilli, deseeded and roughly chopped

2 red peppers, deseeded and roughly chopped

3 garlic cloves, chopped

600g ripe tomatoes, quartered

1 x 400g can of chopped tomatoes

1 litre chicken or vegetable stock

salt and freshly ground black pepper

a few fresh basil leaves, to garnish

a few spoonfuls of tapenade, to serve

A few hours before you plan to serve this soup, put the olive oil into a shallow freezer-proof tray and freeze.

In a large pot, combine the vegetable oil, onion, chilli, peppers and garlic and cook, stirring occasionally, for 5 minutes. Add the fresh tomatoes, season lightly and cook for a few minutes more.

Stir in the tinned tomatoes and the stock and bring to the boil, stirring regularly to ensure nothing burns and sticks on the bottom. Lower the heat and simmer gently for 30 minutes.

Remove from the heat and purée until super-smooth. Taste and adjust the seasoning. If you want it really smooth, strain through a sieve. Refrigerate until well chilled.

Just before serving, ladle the soup into bowls. To float the olive oil on top, scrape at the frozen oil with a spoon to get shavings and add dollops of this to the soup in the bowls. Throw in some tapenade, and add a few basil leaves to garnish, then serve.

BEETROOT
KETCHUP
BALSAMIC
FETA

SERVES 4

This is real home cooking, based on my wife's family recipe – because, when it comes to soup making, she is the star. This recipe is straightforward and everyone loves it, thanks to the secret, traditional Polish ingredient: ketchup. What's more, if you keep vacuum-packed beets in the fridge, this is basically a store-cupboard recipe that requires almost no skill other than the ability to use a blender. Minimum effort, maximum effect; try it and you will see.

1 large onion, roughly chopped
1 garlic clove, bashed
1 tablespoon vegetable oil
600g beetroot, cooked and coarsely chopped
150ml ketchup
a splash of balsamic vinegar
1.2 litres chicken or vegetable stock or water
salt and freshly ground black pepper
40g feta cheese, crumbled
a small bunch of fresh basil or mint
extra virgin olive oil, for drizzling

In a large pan, cook the onion and garlic in the vegetable oil until soft.

Add the beetroot, ketchup, balsamic and stock or water and simmer for 20–30 minutes. Taste and adjust the seasoning.

Blitz with a hand-held blender until smooth-ish.

Garnish with the feta, basil or mint leaves and olive oil, then serve.

DILL PICKLES
POTATO
SMOKED SAUSAGE
BACON

What is in a name? Quite a lot, apparently. When we first started serving this soup, I mistakenly called it pickled cucumber soup, which was not met with great enthusiasm from customers. So now we call it Polish potato soup with sausage and bacon, and there has never been a bad word said. In fact, it is one of our most popular soups. This recipe comes from my assistant chef Marcin, a talented, patient, hard-working chap. Like this recipe, he is a gem.

175g dill pickles, grated
125ml pickling brine
1 leek, finely chopped
2 stalks of celery, grated
1 large carrot, well scrubbed and grated
3 large potatoes, well scrubbed and diced
125g smoked air-cured Polish sausage, diced
75g bacon, finely chopped
1 litre water
½ a bunch of fresh dill, chopped
250ml single cream
zest of 1 orange
salt and coarsely ground black pepper

In a large pan, combine all the ingredients, except the dill, cream and orange zest and bring just to the boil. Lower the heat and cook very gently for 3 hours, uncovered.

Just before serving, add the remaining ingredients and stir. Taste, adjust the seasoning and serve.

CAULIFLOWER CUMIN BAY LEAF CREAM

SERVES 4–6

2 small cauliflowers, separated into florets
4 sprigs of fresh thyme
3–4 garlic cloves, bashed and peeled
2 onions, finely chopped
30ml vegetable oil
20g cumin seeds
1 litre vegetable stock
2 bay leaves
salt and freshly ground black pepper
250ml double cream (optional)

Preheat the oven to 200°C/gas mark 6. Line one or two baking trays with baking parchment.

Put the cauliflower, thyme, garlic, onions, oil and cumin seeds into a large bowl and toss well to combine. Spread in a single layer on the prepared baking trays and roast until golden and just charring, 20–30 minutes.

Transfer to a large pan. Add the stock and bay leaves and bring to the boil, then lower the heat and simmer for 30 minutes.

Remove the bay leaves, then taste and adjust the seasoning. Serve as it is, or blend until smooth and add cream as desired.

Roasting heightens the flavour of both the cauliflower and the cumin, and they partner one another so well that it is best not to add too much more, so I've left this simple. Sometimes I blend this soup, sometimes I don't. I am equally undecided about adding cream – sometimes I do that too. It all depends on mood and you should do the same.

SMOKED BACON PORK RIB ALLSPICE SAUERKRAUT POTATO

SERVES 4–6

300g smoked bacon, chopped

500g pork rib, on the bone, cut into 4–6 portions

1 onion, cut into half-moon slices

4 garlic cloves, bashed

1 teaspoon ground allspice

600g sauerkraut, rinsed and drained

200g potatoes, diced

10g dried mushrooms

1 carrot, sliced

2 teaspoons ground cumin

1 teaspoon salt

1 teaspoon coarsely ground black pepper

4 bay leaves

2 litres chicken or vegetable stock or water

In a stockpot, cook the bacon over a low heat to render the fat. Add the pork ribs, onion and garlic and cook, stirring occasionally, until the onion is just translucent.

Add the remaining ingredients and bring to the boil over a medium-high heat. Skim off any foam that rises to the surface, then lower the heat, cover and simmer for 45–60 minutes. Serve.

I came across this soup in the mountains of Poland, on a long walk in freezing weather, with my future wife. It was December and we were on our way to see a lake surrounded by snow-capped peaks. Halfway there, we stopped at a little wooden shack, literally, for lunch. There was no menu, you took what you got, and what we got was this. Forget the amazing scenery and the beautiful woman opposite, I was in love with the soup. When the restorative powers of the sauerkraut kicked in, I came to my senses and remembered to notice the woman. This is fantastic; try it.

MAINS 4

FISH

SALMON
CORIANDER
MINT
WALNUT
HUMMUS

The inspiration for this came from a recipe I saw for a pasta salad with salmon and hummus. The combination really resonates, because of the Middle Eastern vibe with a sort of wacky Australian-hybrid approach. Ultimately, though, it is a London creation, because it really came together when I first opened Chriskitch. It is a menu standard and a customer favourite. If I had a signature dish, this might be the one.

SERVES 10-12

4kg boneless, skin-on salmon fillet
zest and juice of 1–2 lemons
200g fresh coriander, leaves picked
120g fresh mint, leaves picked and
    roughly chopped
300g walnuts, severely roasted and
    coarsely chopped (see *Note* on page 17)
2 teaspoons sumac
seeds from 1 pomegranate
180g hummus
1 red onion, finely chopped
about 150ml extra virgin olive oil

FOR THE DRESSING
1 garlic clove, finely chopped
1 teaspoon salt
200g natural yoghurt
200ml tahini
juice of 3 lemons
salt and freshly ground black pepper

For the dressing, put the garlic, salt, yoghurt and tahini into a bowl and stir to blend. Add enough lemon juice to thin to the consistency of pouring cream. Taste and adjust the seasoning. Refrigerate until needed.

Preheat the oven to 180°C/gas mark 4 and line a baking tray with baking parchment.

Place the salmon on the baking tray and roast until almost cooked through – about 15–20 minutes. Remove from the oven and leave to cool to room temperature.

Meanwhile, set aside a small amount of the lemon zest, coriander and mint to decorate. Put the walnuts, lemon juice, remaining zest and herbs, sumac and half the pomegranate seeds into a bowl, mix well and set aside.

Put the salmon on a serving platter and pour the dressing over. Spread over the hummus, then the walnut and herb mixture. Scatter over the reserved herbs, lemon zest and pomegranate seeds, and drizzle over as much oil as you like. Serve.

I suppose many people can attribute their own awakening, culinary or otherwise, to one forward-thinking individual, and I owe mine to chef Glenn Bacon back in Australia. Whenever I see white poppy seeds I think of him. The way he approached food, at the time, was really out there and his influence contributed so much to my cooking style.

SERVES 6–8

1 x 800g side of salmon, skinless and trimmed
salt and freshly ground black pepper
100g white poppy seeds
30g black lumpfish caviar
a pinch of sumac

FOR THE CUCUMBER SALAD

20g capers
20g caper berries
1 small red onion, thinly sliced
1 small fennel bulb, thinly sliced
a small bunch of fresh dill, chopped
40g baby spinach leaves
zest of ½ an orange
juice of 1 orange
1 large cucumber, thinly sliced into rounds
40ml extra virgin olive oil

FOR THE HOT SMOKE MIXTURE

10g jasmine tea leaves
15g soft dark brown sugar
zest of ½ an orange
½ a cinnamon stick
3 star anise, roughly broken
100g uncooked jasmine rice
3 green cardamom pods

SALMON
WHITE POPPY SEEDS
FENNEL
ORANGE
CUCUMBER

Season the salmon, then set aside.

Preheat the oven to 200°C/gas mark 6 and line a flameproof roasting tin with foil. Set the salmon on a wire rack that will fit inside the tray.

Combine all the salad ingredients in a mixing bowl, toss well and set aside.

Put the hot smoke mixture ingredients in the prepared tin and mix around to blend and spread out evenly. Set the tin over a high heat until it starts smoking. Turn off the heat and quickly set the salmon on the wire rack over the smoke mixture. Cover the whole thing tightly with 2 layers of foil so that no smoke can escape. Put in the oven until just cooked, about 10 minutes.

Remove from the oven, uncover and lift out the rack with the salmon. Set aside to cool until just warm. When cooled, sprinkle over the poppy seeds in a thick, even light crust on the top. (The salmon can be prepared to this point up to 2 days ahead and refrigerated – return to room temperature to serve.)

To serve, slice the salmon into portions and set on plates. Top with a mound of salad and a dollop of lumpfish, and scatter over some sumac.

Note: See page 142 for more on tea smoking.

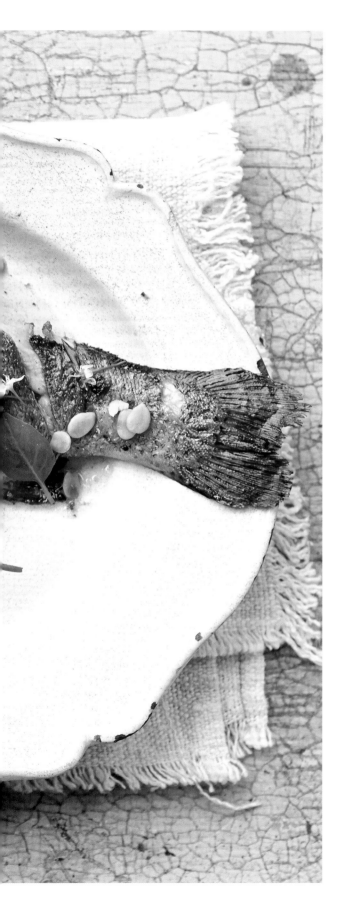

SEA BASS
MANDARIN SALT
SPRING ONION
CHIVES

You cannot beat a whole fish for spectacular presentation and, kitchen-wise, it is also easy on the chef; just season and cook. This then leaves time for reflection. As a result, I decided to swap the usual lemon-fish alliance for mandarin. It is subtle, straightforward and achieves that 'something different' effect I always strive for. If watermelon seeds are difficult to find, use sesame seeds instead.

SERVES 4

4 whole sea bass, cleaned, gutted and skin scored
60g Mandarin Salt (see page 217)
100ml extra virgin olive oil
25g unsalted butter
2 spring onions, diagonally sliced
a small bunch of fresh chives, preferably with flowers
60g watermelon seeds, toasted
a few sprigs of fresh thyme and baby basil

Season the fish all over with the mandarin salt.

In a large non-stick frying pan, heat a few tablespoons of the oil. When hot, add the fish and cook for 3–5 minutes per side. Best to work in batches and cook two at a time.

Transfer the cooked fish to a serving plate. Add the butter to the hot pan, and when sizzling pour over the fish.

Scatter over the spring onions, chives, watermelon seeds, thyme and basil, and serve.

COD
CANNELLINI BEANS
MINT
CHAMOMILE

SERVES 6

Confit is a technique for cooking meat very, very slowly in fat. But it is also a way of making sure your finished dish is flaky and moist, which can be difficult to achieve when pan frying or baking fish.

1 teaspoon salt

2 garlic cloves, bashed

1 teaspoon fennel seeds

1 teaspoon black peppercorns

1 teaspoon dried mint

1 teaspoon dried oregano

1 teaspoon dried basil

900g boneless skinless cod (allow 150g per portion),
   or other white fish

vegetable oil, for marinating, about 500 ml

a small bunch of fresh mint, leaves stripped

extra virgin olive oil

Chamomile Salt (see page 217)

Mint Sugar (see page 217)

freshly ground black pepper

FOR THE BEANS

zest and juice of 1 lemon

2 x 400g cans of cannellini beans, drained

125ml extra virgin olive oil

3 garlic cloves

½ teaspoon ground cumin

Combine the salt, garlic, fennel seeds, peppercorns, mint, oregano and basil in a large shallow baking dish. Add the fish pieces and toss in the mixture to coat evenly. Pour over just enough vegetable oil to coat completely. The longer you leave this now the better, but you can also make it last minute. If you have time, a few hours, covered, in the fridge is ideal. Return it to room temperature before placing in the oven.

Preheat the oven to 70°C/gas mark as low as possible. Roast the fish for 30 minutes, then remove from the oven and let the residual heat of the oil finish cooking it for a further 30 minutes.

Meanwhile, prepare the beans. Put 4 tablespoons of the lemon juice and all the other ingredients except the lemon zest into a blender and whizz until smooth. Transfer to a pan and taste. Adjust for seasoning and lemonyness, then cover and set aside until needed.

When ready to serve, gently reheat the beans. In a small bowl, toss the mint leaves in the olive oil.

To serve, place a good dollop of bean purée on each plate. Lift a piece of cod out of the oil and set on top of the beans. Sprinkle with some chamomile salt, a drizzle of the cooking oil, a pinch of Mint Sugar and a grind of black pepper.

MEAT

I love dried mango powder and am always looking for ways to incorporate it into my cooking. After some experimentation, I discovered that amchur (dried mango powder) and pork are like two best friends who haven't quite met yet – but now that I've introduced them, they are inseparable, at least in my kitchen. Here they team up with pork's traditional partner, apple, and a good whack of chilli-ginger spice heat and some balsamic for tang. A very successful encounter.

PORK
DRIED MANGO POWDER
GINGER
APPLE
DATES

SERVES 4–6

1.2–1.4kg pork loin, rindless
100ml honey
80g soft dark brown sugar
80g amchur powder (dried mango powder)
100g fresh ginger, peeled and grated
2 fresh red chillies, deseeded and sliced
5 apples, preferably Cox's
120g dried dates, pitted
2 large red onions, thickly sliced
200ml balsamic vinegar
3 cinnamon sticks

Preheat the oven to 220°C/gas mark 7.

Score the fat layer on the pork in a criss-cross pattern, trying not to cut into the meat. Set aside.

In a bowl, combine the honey, brown sugar, mango powder, ginger and chillies and stir to combine. Rub this mixture into the pork, massaging it all over to distribute it evenly.

Core the apples and stuff with the dates. Set aside.

Arrange the onion slices in a roasting tray and set the apples on top. Place the pork in the tray and splash the balsamic over all, throw in the cinnamon and put into the oven. Immediately reduce the heat to 180°C/gas mark 4 and roast for about 1 hour. The top of the meat will go crispy and dark.

Remove the pork and cut into slices. Recuperate any pan juice and use it, either drizzled over or served alongside – it is gold dust. Serve with the apples.

PORK BELLY
SOY SAUCE
BLACK GRAPE
MAPLE SYRUP
SWEET POTATO

The thing about Chriskitch food is that everything needs to be quick to prep, gentle on the wallet and cook-ahead. For these reasons, I am partial to a braise, because I simply throw a few things into a pan, let it simmer while I do something else and the result is meltingly delicious food that looks and tastes amazing. Here is just such a dish, where pork belly practically dissolves in a sticky spiced maple-soy reduction. Cheap, easy, yum: all boxes ticked.

SERVES 4

900g pork belly

1 litre chicken stock or water

100ml soy sauce

100ml maple syrup

150g black grapes

1 cinnamon stick

5 star anise

4 garlic cloves, left whole

3cm piece of fresh ginger, peeled

250g soft dark brown sugar

2 fresh red chillies, deseeded and finely chopped

5 tablespoons fish sauce

5 tablespoons fresh lemon juice (about 1 fat lemon)

4 large sweet potatoes, scrubbed and left whole

Greek yoghurt, to serve

dried dates, to serve

One day before serving, trim the pork belly into a slab about 10cm x 6cm. Score the fat side by making a few incisions across the top.

Put an ovenproof casserole over a medium-high heat. When hot, add the pork belly, fat side down, and cook until a deep golden brown. Turn it over and brown the other side.

Add the remaining ingredients, apart from the sweet potatoes, yoghurt and dates, then lower the heat and barely simmer over the lowest heat possible for 4½ hours. Keep an eye and make sure the pork always stays submerged. Remove from the heat and leave to cool in the dish, then cover and refrigerate for at least 12 hours.

The day of serving, preheat the oven to 200°C/gas mark 6 and line a baking tray with baking parchment.

Lift the pork belly out of the broth and set in the middle of the baking tray, skin side up. Put the sweet potatoes around the pork. Roast until the meat is crispy and dark brown on top, 20–30 minutes. Continue roasting the sweet potatoes for a bit longer if necessary.

Meanwhile, put the broth back on the stove and cook over a medium-high heat to reduce until thick and syrupy.

Remove the pork and sweet potatoes from the oven. Dollop the yoghurt on a serving platter and set the pork belly on top. Arrange the sweet potatoes around the pork and drizzle over some of the reduced broth and a few dates. Serve.

Much of the meat cooking we do needs to be make-ahead, so roast beef is a good one, but here is the Chriskitch treatment, which means a good mix of in-your-face herbs and spices with a straightforward cooking method. Because this is a room temperature dish, I serve it with a pomelo salad; something unexpected and fresh to balance as well as complement the meat.

SERVES 4-6

1 tablespoon nigella seeds
zest and juice of 4 limes
1 tablespoon garlic granules
1 tablespoon coriander seeds
2 tablespoons fenugreek seeds
1 teaspoon fine salt
½ teaspoon ground black pepper
5g dried kaffir lime leaves
5g dried curry leaves
3 garlic cloves, bashed and roughly chopped
100ml extra virgin olive oil
1kg beef fillet, or use a ribeye or sirloin joint
a few sprigs of fresh basil
2 limes, halved, to serve

FOR THE SALAD
1 large pomelo or grapefruit
2 red chillies, sliced
1 large bunch of fresh coriander, roughly chopped

BEEF
KAFFIR LIME
CURRY LEAF
POMELO
CHILLI

Put the nigella seeds into a small heatproof bowl, pour over boiling water to cover well and leave to soak for at least 30 minutes. Drain and add the lime juice.

Preheat the oven to 220°C/gas mark 7 and line a baking tray with baking parchment.

Add the rest of the ingredients, apart from the beef, lime zest and basil, to the bowl of nigella seeds and mix well. Rub this mixture into the beef, coating it evenly all over. Set aside at room temperature, covered, to marinate for 30 minutes.

Uncover, then put the beef on the baking tray and roast in the oven. For medium, cook for 30–35 minutes; for well done, 40–45 minutes. Remove from the oven and leave to rest for 15 minutes.

Meanwhile, prepare the salad. Segment the pomelo or grapefruit and put into a bowl. Add the lime zest and chillies and mix well with your hands to combine. Set aside.

When the meat is cooked, slice and arrange on a platter with the limes and basil. Serve with the salad.

Note: If you are going to serve this as part of a buffet, pre-sliced, I recommend cooking it on the well-done side, otherwise the blood leaches out on to the platter and looks unappetizing. But if you are serving it straight away, less cooking time is better.

This is a classic French braise, which I have jazzed up with some fresh ginger, star anise, grape molasses, and a few other bits and pieces. Unlike almost everything else I make, this takes some forward thinking because the tongue needs salting for a few days. If you have never cooked or eaten tongue, start here.

SERVES 4-6

3 lambs' tongues
400g fine salt
1 tablespoon black peppercorns

FOR THE BRAISE

6 bay leaves
60ml grape molasses
50g fresh ginger, sliced
1 tablespoon ground nutmeg
2 garlic bulbs, quartered
4 star anise
2 tablespoons sweet paprika
1 white onion, finely chopped

TO SERVE

2-3 red onions
1kg carrots, peeled and trimmed
salt and freshly ground black pepper
extra virgin olive oil
honey, for drizzling
a few sprigs of fresh thyme

LAMBS' TONGUE
GRAPE MOLASSES
GINGER
STAR ANISE

Three days before you plan on serving, rinse the tongues under cold running water and pat dry. With a small sharp knife, trim away any gristly bits and give the tongues a good scrub.

Choose a non-reactive container large enough to hold the tongues, either glass or plastic. A large sturdy ziplock bag will also work. In the container, combine the tongue with the salt and peppercorns and mix well. It will be dry to start with, but don't worry.

Every day, turn the tongues around in the mixture. On day three, remove the tongues, put them into a colander under cold running water and rinse well to remove all the salt. Pat dry with kitchen paper.

Put the tongues into a small casserole (just large enough to hold them comfortably) and add the braising ingredients. Bring to the boil over a medium heat, then lower the heat, cover and simmer gently for 2–3 hours. Keep an eye and make sure the pan does not dry out. Add a little water if necessary.

Meanwhile, preheat the oven to 180°C/gas mark 4. Arrange the onions, whole and unpeeled, on a baking tray and roast until tender when pierced, 20–30 minutes.

While the onions are roasting, cook the carrots in boiling lightly salted water until just tender, about 15–20 minutes, then drain and set aside.

When the simmering time is up, remove the tongues from the liquid and cool slightly. While still warm, peel off the outer layer. Don't wait until it's fully cooled or this will be difficult.

To serve, slice the tongues thinly and serve in the sauce, accompanied with the onions and carrots. Drizzle over some oil and honey, season lightly and scatter over the thyme sprigs.

CALVES' LIVER
LEEKS
VANILLA
HONEY

SERVES 4–6

70g unsalted butter

4 garlic cloves, bashed and peeled

4–6 plump sprigs of fresh thyme

12 baby leeks, topped and tailed

1 vanilla pod, split

800g calves' liver, cut into 4–6 pieces

1 teaspoon dried pink peppercorns

1 heaped teaspoon sea salt flakes

1 tablespoon vegetable oil

100ml malt vinegar

100ml honey

I think of this combo as beauty and the beast: sweet leeks, pretty delicate vanilla and ugly stinky liver. Not that I think liver is unattractive – I love the stuff but, let's face it, it is difficult to make it look good. So here is an unexpected marriage that works well on both the palate and the eye. I wouldn't be surprised if this lovely sweet-sour number was able to convert a few reluctant liver eaters.

In a non-stick pan, combine the butter, garlic, thyme and leeks. Cook over a medium heat, letting the leeks braise in the butter mixture, for 7–10 minutes.

Remove from the heat. Scrape the vanilla seeds out of the pod and add both seeds and pod to the pan. Stir to combine everything, then set aside.

Season the liver with the peppercorns and salt.

Heat the oil in a large non-stick pan, add the liver pieces and cook over a high heat, 2–3 minutes each side, to sear.

Add the vinegar, stir, scraping up the burnt bits, and cook for no longer than 30 seconds. Add the honey, stir again and turn the liver pieces over in the mixture to coat evenly with the glaze. Remove from the heat.

Divide the leek mixture between plates, top each with a slice of liver and drizzle over the pan juices. Serve.

BEEF CHEEKS
JUNIPER
STAR ANISE
SOY SAUCE

SERVES 4

This is an East meets West slow braise, where traditional European herbs simmer away with Chinese rice wine, star anise and soy. This goes really well with a creamy mash.

3 tablespoons vegetable oil

4 beef cheeks

2 onions, coarsely chopped

1 large carrot, peeled and coarsely chopped

1 celery stalk, coarsely chopped

1 whole garlic bulb, halved, plus an extra
   4 garlic cloves, bashed

a few juniper berries

1 sprig of fresh oregano, leaves stripped

2 bay leaves

3 star anise

3 tablespoons tomato purée

800ml red wine

200ml Chinese rice wine

80ml soy sauce

60g palm sugar (or demerara sugar)

a serious pinch of freshly ground black pepper

mashed potato, to serve

Preheat the oven to 150°C/gas mark 2.

Heat half the oil in a frying pan. Add the beef and cook over a high heat until seared all over. Don't be afraid to let it get a bit charred and dark. Remove the meat and set aside.

To the same pan, add the remaining oil, the onions, carrot, celery and garlic bulb and cloves and cook, stirring occasionally, until deep golden.

In an ovenproof casserole with a lid, combine the remaining ingredients and stir well to mix. Add the beef and onion and carrot mixture, stir again and bring to the boil. Cover and put in the oven to braise for 3–4 hours.

Remove from the oven and take out the meat. With a stick blender (or in a regular blender), purée the cooking liquid into a sexy rich, dark, smooth sauce. Pour this over the meat, serve with mashed potato alongside and wait for the love to come your way.

VEAL
CAPERS
TUNA

Meat and fish is an unlikely combination but this is a traditional Italian recipe, *veal tonnato*, and they know what they are doing, those Italians. It's timeless and perfect and makes a change from the rather overdone buffet table poached salmon or roast beef. This works so well that there is no point in deviating with ingredients, but I prefer to serve mine sliced, rather than whole as is traditional, because it looks so much more appetizing.

1 onion studded with 2 cloves

1kg veal rump

1 carrot

1 stalk of celery

3 garlic cloves, bashed

1 teaspoon fine salt

red pepper flakes (pul biber)

1 teaspoon pumpkin seed oil, for drizzling

cherry tomatoes, to serve

a few sprigs of fresh parsley, leaves torn, to garnish

1 spring onion, thinly sliced, to garnish

FOR THE TONNATO SAUCE

1 x 200g tin of tuna in oil, drained

1 large potato, boiled and peeled

4 anchovy fillets, plus extra to serve

3 tablespoons capers in brine, plus extra to serve

juice and zest of 1 lemon

60ml extra virgin olive oil

200g good-quality mayonnaise

1 teaspoon Dijon mustard

Put the onion into a large stockpot with the veal, carrot, celery, garlic, red pepper flakes and pumpkin seed oil. Pour in cold water to cover by about 4–5 cm.

Bring to the boil over a high heat, then lower the heat and simmer very, very gently for 1½–2 hours. Keep the boil very gentle or the meat will be tough.

Remove the meat from the broth and bring to room temperature, then cover and refrigerate. (Reserve the broth for another use – it can be frozen.)

Put the tuna, potato, anchovies, capers, lemon juice and oil into a food processor and whiz to a paste. Add the mayonnaise and mustard and pulse a few times just to blend them in.

When ready to serve, slice the veal very thinly and arrange on a platter. Top with dollops of the tonnato sauce and throw on the lemon zest, tomatoes (some halved), the extra capers and anchovies, parsley and spring onion.

BEEF MINCE
CANNELLINI BEANS
CORIANDER
LEMON

These are such a good item for the buffet table or for informal entertaining – their size always makes people smile. I suggest to serve these accompanied by lardons and thickly sliced leeks all slowly braised in butter, garlic and thyme.

SERVES 6

1.7kg beef mince

1 x 400g can of cannellini beans, drained

35g sesame seeds

35g linseeds

1 tablespoon fennel seeds

1 tablespoon coriander seeds

1 small bunch of fresh coriander, leaves roughly
    chopped, stems finely chopped

1 red onion, diced

zest and juice of 1 lemon

1 teaspoon nigella seeds

1 teaspoon garlic granules

a pinch of chilli flakes

1 teaspoon ground coriander

2 heaped teaspoons fine salt

1 teaspoon freshly ground black pepper

125g breadcrumbs

2 eggs

2 tablespoons honey

grape molasses, for drizzling

golden syrup, for drizzling

Preheat the oven to 200°C/gas mark 6 and line one or two baking trays with baking parchment.

Put all the ingredients, apart from the grape molasses and golden syrup, into a large mixing bowl. Add 115ml of water and mix well with your hands. Massage gently with your fingers and lightly crush some of the beans.

Using your hands, shape the mixture into balls about the size of a peach (they should weigh about 120g each) and arrange on the baking trays.

Put into the oven and roast until brown and a bit crispy all over. (The meatballs can be made a day or so in advance up to this point; if refrigerated, return them to room temperature before using.)

Just before serving, put as many meatballs as will fit comfortably into your frying pan and drizzle over some grape molasses and a spoonful of golden syrup. Heat until bubbling and turn the meatballs around in the mixture to coat evenly. Serve with the pan juices. These can also be served lukewarm.

BEEF MINCE
FENNEL SEEDS
AUBERGINE
TAHINI

In case anyone needed it, this is proof that not all meatloaves are created equal. My Middle Eastern heritage is fully apparent here, combining so many of the flavours that I love. You could pair this with mash, as per tradition, but it also goes well with grain salads.

SERVES 4-6

750g beef mince

1 tablespoon each fennel and coriander seeds

3 teaspoons each linseeds and sesame seeds

2½ teaspoons each ground cumin, ground coriander and nigella seeds

2 teaspoons each garlic granules and ground cinnamon

1½ teaspoons black mustard seeds

½ teaspoon chilli flakes

1 teaspoon fine sea salt

a good pinch of coarsely ground black pepper

60g raisins

1 small red onion, finely chopped

2 eggs, beaten

170g breadcrumbs

60ml malt vinegar

a few sprigs of fresh dill, finely chopped

2 large aubergines

150ml tahini

1-2 tablespoons honey

a squeeze of lemon juice

100ml natural yoghurt

Put the meat, spices, salt, pepper, raisins, onion, eggs, breadcrumbs, vinegar and dill into a large mixing bowl and mix well. Cover and leave to stand at room temperature for at least 30 minutes, or refrigerate for up to 2 hours.

Preheat the oven to 180°C/gas mark 4 and line a 900g non-stick loaf tin with baking parchment.

Slice the aubergines very thinly lengthways. Heat a large non-stick frying pan and add the aubergine slices. Working in batches, cook until just golden on each side, setting them aside as they are done.

Line the loaf tin with the aubergine slices so that they overlap one another and also hang over the sides.

Press the meat mixture into the tin and fold the overhanging aubergine slices over the top. Bake until cooked through, about 1½ hours. Leave to cool slightly, then turn out.

Mix together the tahini, honey and lemon juice. Taste and adjust the seasoning. Swirl in the yoghurt, or keep separate, and serve with the meatloaf.

LAMB
LINSEEDS
ROSEMARY
HONEY

SERVES 4

The flavours of this dish come together at the last minute, when you add the honey and rosemary to the pan. The heat melts the honey and it forms a sticky glaze for the seed-crusted chops. Nutty meets sweet meets herbal. Serve with a purée of some sort, something velvety smooth like beans or potatoes, to get a contrast of textures as well.

8–12 lamb cutlets, bones well trimmed

100g self-raising flour

salt and freshly ground black pepper

3 eggs

60ml milk

100g golden linseeds

100g brown linseeds

40g unsalted butter

80ml vegetable oil

1 tablespoon finely chopped fresh rosemary leaves

1–2 sprigs of fresh rosemary

50ml honey

Using a meat mallet (or the bottom of a heavy pot, which is what I use), lightly pound out the meat to flatten it slightly. You don't want the cutlets too thin, just to even them out a bit for better heat distribution and also to compensate for the size, as they will shrink after cooking.

Arrange your coating mixture: put the flour on a plate and mix in a good pinch of salt and pepper. In a bowl, beat together the eggs, milk and a splash of water. Put the light and dark linseeds on separate plates.

To assemble, work with one cutlet at a time and use one hand for dipping in the flour and the other for the egg and linseeds afterwards, otherwise both hands get coated as well as the lamb. Dip one cutlet into the flour on both sides and tap off the excess. Then dip it into the egg, coating it on both sides,

and let the excess drip away a bit. Finally, dip it into the linseed mix, on both sides, pressing down to help the seeds coat and adhere. Set aside on a tray and continue until all the cutlets are coated.

In a large non-stick pan, heat the butter and oil over a medium-high heat until sizzling and blended. Add the cutlets and cook for 3–4 minutes per side. You may need to use two pans, or work in batches, if your pan is not large enough. Transfer the cooked cutlets to a clean platter.

Lower the heat, add the chopped rosemary, sprigs and honey to the pan and stir to combine. Return the lamb to the pan and cook for about 1 minute each side, turning halfway to coat in the rosemary and honey mix. Transfer to a platter and serve, scraping any juices from the pan over all.

LAMB SHOULDER
CARDAMOM PODS
TREACLE
COFFEE
APPLE

Nothing but a pot-roast, this one, except it has some complex spicing going on, so it does not taste like an everyday roast. The treacle and coffee give a dark black crust, which is why I like to pair it with the crisp white apple salad. Not only does this add some tang, visually it brightens the plate and looks good. A really silky, creamy mash partners well with this.

Preheat the oven to 180°C/gas mark 4.

Using a pestle and mortar, grind together the cloves and cardamom seeds. Put all the spices into a large bowl and stir to blend.

Add the marinade ingredients and stir, then massage the marinade into the lamb, all over evenly. Leave to marinate for 10 minutes. Put the lamb into an ovenproof casserole, put the lid on and roast for 3 hours.

Just before serving, prepare the salad. Put the lemon juice into a bowl. Thinly slice the apples, whole, using a mandoline, and put the slices straight into the bowl with the lemon juice. Pick the mint leaves off the stems and add to the bowl with the apples. Throw in a handful of lemon zest and the almonds. Add a good drizzle of olive oil and toss gently, then drizzle with the honey. Serve the lamb immediately, with the apple mint salad.

SERVES 4–6

2 cloves
seeds from 2 green cardamom pods
a pinch of ground cloves
2 teaspoons ground cinnamon
1 tablespoon fennel seeds
a pinch of chilli flakes
1.1kg boneless lamb shoulder

FOR THE COFFEE MARINADE
100ml black treacle
3 tablespoons instant coffee
30g whole almonds, coarsely chopped
1 teaspoon vanilla extract
40ml balsamic vinegar
1 tablespoon fish sauce or 2 tinned anchovies,
   finely chopped

FOR THE SALAD
zest and juice of 1 lemon
4 Cox's apples
a few sprigs of fresh mint
a handful of whole almonds, severely roasted
   (see *Note* on page 17)
extra virgin olive oil
80g honey, for drizzling

DUCK LEG
PLUM
POMEGRANATE
STAR ANISE

SERVES 4

Deep burgundy hues and plummy spiced pomegranate gorgeousness. Although this is dead easy to throw together, the cook will have already done enough, so diners beware plum stones.

4 duck legs
salt

FOR THE MARINADE
300g fresh plums, with stones, or use frozen plums, defrosted
125g whole pitted prunes
80g pomegranate seeds
100ml pomegranate molasses
4 star anise
1 cinnamon stick
zest peeled in wide strips and juice of 1 large orange
50ml honey
50ml balsamic vinegar
50ml apple cider
2 fresh red chillies, deseeded and sliced
1 scant teaspoon Sichuan peppercorns, coarsely crushed

Put all the marinade ingredients into a large bowl and stir to combine. Transfer to a non-reactive container just large enough to hold the marinade and the duck legs, or use a large ziplock bag. Add the duck legs and leave to marinate in the fridge overnight, or for at least 6 hours.

Preheat the oven to 140°C/gas mark 1.

Transfer the duck legs and their marinade to a roasting pan. Roast for about 2 hours until the duck turns a deep dark colour and the sauce thickens. Turn the legs halfway through cooking and check for doneness after 1½ hours.

Season the duck legs lightly with salt before serving, at room temperature.

tea smoking

This is a great cooking technique to use, not only because the flavour is fantastic but because it doesn't take up valuable oven space, which is certainly an issue in my kitchen! At Chriskitch I have been known to use a cardboard box and tea lights as a smoker, but I would not recommend you try that at home. A wok with a circular rack and lined with foil is perfect for home smoking. Loads of ingredients lend themselves to tea smoking, but especially poultry and seafood.

DUCK
SOY SAUCE
GREEN TEA

SERVES 4–6

4–6 duck breasts, fat scored
100ml sweet soy sauce
20ml fish sauce
60ml honey
20ml sesame seeds
a pinch of Sichuan peppercorns

FOR THE HOT SMOKE MIXTURE

10g green tea
15g soft dark brown sugar
zest of ½ an orange
½ a cinnamon stick
3 star anise, coarsely broken
100g uncooked jasmine rice
3 green cardamom pods

TO SERVE

4 spring onions, thinly sliced on the diagonal
1 red chilli, sliced
½ a bunch of fresh coriander, leaves picked
honey, for drizzling

Preheat the oven to 200°C/gas 6 and line a wok with 2 layers of foil.

Put the duck breasts, soy sauce, fish sauce, honey, sesame seeds and peppercorns into a mixing bowl. Toss well and set aside.

Add the hot smoke mixture ingredients to the wok, stir gently to combine and set the wok over a high heat until it starts smoking. Set the rack in position – it should sit above the hot smoke mixture – then put the marinated duck on the rack, skin side up.

Lower the heat and cover the whole thing with another sheet of foil and seal the edges so that no smoke escapes. Let it smoke for 15 minutes, then uncover and remove the duck. Dampen the hot mixture before discarding.

Heat a non-stick frying pan. When hot, add the duck breasts skin side down and cook for 3 minutes, then turn them over and cook for 3 minutes on the other side. Remove from the heat, leave to stand for a minute or so, then slice thinly.

Arrange the sliced duck on plates, scatter over the spring onions, chilli and coriander and drizzle with honey. Serve.

CHICKEN
TOMATO
PARMESAN
OLIVE
GARLIC

In a restaurant kitchen, perhaps more than at home, we end up with lots of Parmesan rinds, which I do not like to discard unused. Here the rind adds depth and richness to the delicate milk poaching broth for a soothing and simple chicken dish. The olives add a salty punch and colour contrast, just enough but not too much. This is essentially gentle, and that is precisely why I love it.

1.5 litres milk
a big chunk of Parmesan cheese rind, about 150g
4 garlic cloves, bashed
4 large sprigs of fresh thyme
2 bay leaves
2 onions, quartered
4–6 chicken supremes, with skin (1 per portion)
4–6 tomatoes (1 per portion)
1 tablespoon rock salt
200g black olives, with stones
extra virgin olive oil, to finish

Preheat the oven to 90°C/gas mark as low as possible.

In a large ovenproof casserole, combine the milk, Parmesan rind, garlic, thyme, bay leaves and onions. Add the chicken. Cover with a lid, transfer to the oven and cook for 1 hour and 10 minutes.

Meanwhile, prepare the tomatoes. Line a baking tray with baking parchment. Make a circular incision all the way around the outside of each tomato in a spiral, then arrange the tomatoes on the tray and set aside until needed.

Remove the chicken from the oven, add the salt and olives and return to the oven for a further 30 minutes. Remove from the oven.

To serve, put one chicken piece, a few onion quarters and one tomato on each plate. Ladle over some of the cooking broth, drizzle over a little olive oil and serve.

CHICKEN
BROWN SUGAR
BALSAMIC VINEGAR
CHILLI
ROSEMARY

SERVES 4

This mix uses equal amounts of
balsamic and sugar, so the sweet-
tart taste balances beautifully
in the crisp, caramelized crust
that forms on the skin. Because
there is so much balsamic, the
quality is really important
here. Use the good stuff. Fresh
rosemary, a whopping great
big bunch, is also key because
you want that blast of flavour
from the essential oils in the
fresh leaves.

250g soft dark brown sugar

250ml best-quality balsamic vinegar

a really big bunch of fresh rosemary, roughly chopped,
   including stalks, plus a few extra sprigs

100g raisins

2 fresh red chillies, deseeded and finely chopped

1 teaspoon ground cinnamon

1 tablespoon garlic granules

2 teaspoons salt

1 teaspoon freshly ground black pepper

2 red onions, thickly sliced – peel can stay

1 large free-range chicken, about 1.3kg

Preheat the oven to 160°C/gas mark 3.

With a blender or a stick blender, combine all the
ingredients except the onions, chicken and rosemary
sprigs. Whizz until blended; the mixture does not have to
be smooth.

In an ovenproof casserole large enough to hold the chicken
comfortably, arrange the onion slices. Set the chicken on
top. Pour over the balsamic mixture and spread around
with your hands, massaging it into the chicken all over,
then add the rosemary sprigs.

Cover with a lid, transfer to the oven and roast for 2 hours,
no turning required. Exceptionally large chickens may
take a bit longer, but this should usually be adequate time
to ensure the bird is fully cooked. When you pierce the
thickest part of the thigh with a skewer, the juices should
run clear.

QUAIL
NASHI PEAR
STAR ANISE

This calls for a Chinese master stock which is a bit like a sourdough starter; you are meant to keep re-using it and it improves with time. The idea is to strain it after each use, then refrigerate and return it to the boil at least once a week. You could also freeze it. There are many recipes: below is my version. The ingredients list is long, but this is a simple dish to make.

SERVES 4–6

20ml Chinese rice wine

50g caster sugar

2 nashi pears, peeled, cored and diced

2 red peppers, diced

4–6 quail

2 tablespoons vegetable oil

10ml sweet soy sauce

FOR THE MASTER STOCK

2 litres water

300ml light soy sauce

600ml Chinese rice wine

60g fresh ginger, sliced

8 garlic cloves

3 green cardamom pods

1 piece of cassia bark

peel of 2 mandarins

1 fresh red chilli, deseeded and halved

1 tablespoon cloves

8 star anise

½ tablespoon Sichuan peppercorns

½ tablespoon cumin seeds

1 tablespoon fennel seeds

300ml honey

100g Chinese rock sugar

To make the master stock, put all the ingredients into a large pan and bring to the boil, then lower the heat and simmer, uncovered, for 30 minutes. Set aside.

Put the wine and sugar into a pan, bring to the boil and cook until the sugar dissolves, 1–2 minutes. Add the pears and peppers and return to the boil, then remove from the heat immediately and let the pears and peppers stand for about 15 minutes until tender. Set aside.

Return the master stock to the boil, then add the quail. Leave for 2 minutes, just until the stock returns to the boil, then remove from the heat and leave to stand until cooked through, 10–20 minutes depending on desired doneness.

Remove the quail from the stock and pat dry, then cut them in half.

Heat the oil in a large non-stick frying pan. Add the halved quail pieces, skin side down, and sear over a high heat for a few minutes until crispy.

To serve, spoon some of the pear mixture on to a plate and top with the quail. Drizzle the with sweet soy and serve.

LAMB RIB
YOGHURT
CARDAMOM PODS
GARAM MASALA

SERVES 4

This marinates overnight in a spiced yoghurt mixture both to intensify the flavour, as is the purpose of any marinade, but also to tenderize the meat, which is what the yoghurt does. When it comes to the cooking, the yoghurt will split with the heat, but don't worry, it's OK to break the rules and let it curdle. I am in the flavour business and happy to go off piste in the name of deliciousness. In any case, to date, there have not been any complaints about this; quite the opposite.

280g Greek style yoghurt

½ teaspoon ground turmeric

4–6 green cardamom pods, bruised

½ teaspoon ground cinnamon

2 teaspoons cumin seeds

4 cloves

1 teaspoon ground ginger

½ teaspoon garam masala

2 bay leaves

1.4kg lamb ribs, cut into 4 portions

ghee or vegetable oil, for cooking

80g shelled pistachios

a handful of fresh coriander and mint leaves, roughly torn

1 fresh red chilli, deseeded and sliced, to serve

One day before serving, put the yoghurt, spices and bay leaves into a dish that will fit into your fridge and stir to blend well. Add the ribs, stir to coat thoroughly, then cover and refrigerate overnight.

The day of serving, preheat the oven to 160°C/ gas mark 3.

Transfer the ribs and marinade to an ovenproof pot. Add a little water so that the ribs are barely submerged, and stir to mix. Cover, then set over a medium heat, stirring occasionally, until the liquid just boils. Transfer to the oven, covered, and cook for 1½–2 hours. Remove from the oven.

In a large non-stick pan, heat a thin layer of ghee or vegetable oil. When hot, remove the ribs from the sauce, add to the pan and fry to crisp them up. Don't worry if the sauce looks curdled – it's fine.

Put the pistachios and herbs on a platter and toss together. Mound the ribs on top, scraping the burnt bits from the pan over the ribs and then pouring over the sauce. Scatter over the chilli and serve.

RABBIT
MUSTARD
TURNIP
PARMESAN
PANCETTA

SERVES 4–6

A simple, classic braise that pairs baby turnips with rabbit. This is elegant yet simple, and it's something I love to cook and serve. I use the whole rabbit when I make this, including the liver and the kidneys, which means some lucky diners get a bonus surprise on their plates.

100ml malt vinegar

150ml water

1 rabbit, cut into 4–6 pieces

salt and freshly ground black pepper

75ml extra virgin olive oil

100ml dry white wine

5 baby carrots, scrubbed

3–4 baby red onions, peeled

4 garlic cloves, sliced

2 bay leaves

4 sage leaves

a few sprigs of fresh rosemary

a small bunch of fresh parsley, chopped, plus extra to serve

juice of 1 lemon

40g Dijon mustard

500ml chicken stock

50g sugar

100g baby turnips, peeled

75g Parmesan cheese, grated

4 slices of pancetta, preferably well aged

Put the vinegar and water into a large non-reactive bowl and add the rabbit. Cover and refrigerate overnight. This helps to tenderize the meat.

The day of serving, preheat the oven to 180°C/gas mark 4. Remove the rabbit from the liquid and pat dry. Season well all over.

In a large ovenproof casserole, heat the oil. When hot, add the rabbit and sear, turning to brown the pieces evenly. Add the wine, carrots, onions and garlic and stir well. Leave to simmer together for about 10 minutes.

Add the herbs, lemon juice, mustard, stock and sugar, and bring to the boil. Add the turnips.

Cover, transfer to the oven and reduce the heat to 160°C/gas mark 3. Braise gently for 1–1 ½ hours.

Remove from the oven and raise the heat to 200°C/gas mark 6. Line a baking tray with baking parchment and scatter over the Parmesan in an even layer. Bake in the oven to melt the cheese and form a big crispy sheet, about 5 minutes. Remove and leave to cool.

Meanwhile, in a non-stick frying pan, cook the pancetta over a medium heat until crispy. Remove.

To serve, dish the rabbit on to plates and top with some of the crispy pancetta and Parmesan chips.

VEGETABLES

CAULIFLOWER
BLUE CHEESE
WALNUT
DRIED LASAGNE

SERVES 8-10

An unexpected combo that never fails to please my vegetarian customers. It's always lasagne for them, but this is a welcome change from the usual offering. The cook benefits too, because this is much quicker to pull together as there is no tomato sauce to simmer first.

28 sheets of dried lasagne

2 medium cauliflowers, grated, plus the tender inner leaves, chopped

200g walnuts, roughly chopped, plus extra to garnish

200g raisins

400g Cheddar cheese, grated

200g blue cheese, Stilton or other, crumbled

a handful of pumpkin seeds

FOR THE BÉCHAMEL SAUCE

2 litres full-fat milk

200g plain flour

200g unsalted butter

1 teaspoon salt

a pinch of freshly ground black pepper

a pinch of freshly grated nutmeg

For the béchamel, heat the milk to just below boiling and set aside. Combine the flour and butter in a pan and cook over a medium heat, stirring constantly until sandy in texture, then take off the heat.

Bring the milk back to just below boiling. Add the salt, pepper and nutmeg. Put the roux back over a low heat and pour on the hot milk gradually, stirring with a whisk, until the sauce thickens. Remove from the heat and set aside.

Preheat the oven to 180°C/gas mark 4.

Spread a spoonful of béchamel over the bottom of a baking dish and top with a single layer of lasagne sheets (use about 7 sheets per layer). Next, top this with about a quarter of the béchamel, spread evenly. Top this with one-third of the cauliflower and a few leaves, walnuts and raisins, and sprinkle over a quarter of the cheeses. Continue until all the cauliflower has been used up. Finish with a final layer of lasagne sheets and top with the rest of the béchamel and cheese. Scatter some pumpkin seeds over the top.

Bake until golden brown, 30–40 minutes. Let the lasagne cool almost completely before garnishing with walnuts and thyme and cutting it into serving-sized pieces.

frittata

The key to a frittata is long, slow cooking and gentle blending at the outset – these are not scrambled eggs, so don't beat anything. I use an induction hob so that the parchment-lined pans go easily from hob to oven, but if you have a gas hob, use a large parchment-lined baking dish and cook in the oven only.

SERVES 4–6

10ml milk

50ml double cream

10 eggs

50g cream cheese

75g mild Cheddar cheese, grated

salt and freshly ground black pepper

toppings of your choice (I use a combination of
    portobello mushrooms; broccoli; red peppers;
    tomatoes; roasted butternut squash; roasted carrots;
    goat's cheese; watermelon seeds and sesame seeds)

Preheat the oven to 90°C/gas mark as low as possible, and line mini ovenproof frying pans or a baking dish (see above) with baking parchment.

Put the milk, cream, eggs, cheeses, salt and pepper into a large mixing bowl and stir carefully, just enough to blend. Transfer to your pans or baking dish and add any toppings you like.

If using an induction hob, turn the heat to low and cook gently for 10 minutes to set the frittatas a bit (omit this step if you have a gas hob).

Put the pans or the baking dish in the oven and cook for 45–60 minutes until set. Insert a knife into the middle – there should not be any liquid left, but if there is, cook for a bit longer. Remove from the oven to cool, then slice and serve.

156

PUMPKIN
PANEER
PICKLED WALNUT
VINE LEAVES

This is a lasagne of sorts –
without the pasta, but it is a
lasagne in spirit. The pumpkin
and squash mingle with the tang
of the vine leaves, while the
cheese and béchamel soften the
pickled walnuts and chunks of
paneer add texture. This is
adored by vegetarians and meat-
eaters alike.

SERVES 6–8

20–25 vine leaves, in brine, drained and patted dry
500g long-grain rice, cooked
1.3kg pumpkin (Crown Prince squash), peeled and thinly sliced
500g butternut squash, thinly sliced
200g cavolo nero, finely chopped
a few sprigs of fresh thyme
5 sweet potatoes, scrubbed and thinly sliced
200g Cheddar cheese, grated
2 x 225g packets paneer, grated
1 x 390g jar pickled walnuts (or see page 218), drained
   or 100g walnut pieces
salt and freshly ground black pepper

FOR THE BÉCHAMEL SAUCE
700ml full-fat milk
3 bay leaves
50g plain flour
50g unsalted butter
1 teaspoon fine sea salt
a pinch of freshly ground black pepper
a pinch of freshly grated nutmeg

For the béchamel, heat the milk to just below
boiling, add the bay leaves and set aside. Combine
the flour and butter in another saucepan and cook
over a medium heat, stirring constantly, until sandy
in texture, then take off the heat.

Bring the milk to just below boiling and season
with salt, pepper and nutmeg. Put the roux back
over a low heat and pour on the hot milk gradually,
stirring with a whisk, until the sauce thickens.
Remove from the heat and set aside.

Preheat the oven to 180°C/gas mark 4.

Line the bottom of a 33cm cast-iron baking dish
with vine leaves, leaving enough overhanging to
cover the top. On top of the vine leaf base, spread
one-third of béchamel in an even layer, then
add one-third of each ingredient in this order:
cooked rice, pumpkin, squash, kale, both cheeses
and walnuts. Top with 5–6 of the remaining vine
leaves, then repeat the layers until you have 3 layers
of everything in total, finishing by folding the
overhanging leaves over the top and covering any
exposed space with more vine leaves.

Bake until browned, about 60–70 minutes. Serve.

PARSNIPS
PARMESAN
POLENTA
TARRAGON
LIME

This is how I get my kids to eat something other than chips and it's a winner. The grilled limes are, admittedly, a cheffy flourish, but they are very easy to make (you can cook them while the parsnips are roasting) and add heaps in terms of flavour. Pink peppercorns are also an extravagance, but they look so good I can't help myself; use black if that is what you have on hand. This is a definite crowd-pleaser.

SERVES 4–6

100ml vegetable oil

2 limes, halved

400g parsnips, washed and patted dry

100g self-raising flour

2 large eggs

50ml milk, preferably full-fat

100g polenta

100g Parmesan cheese, grated

½ a fresh red chilli, deseeded and sliced

a pinch of dried pink peppercorns, coarsely crushed

sea salt flakes

1 large sprig of fresh tarragon, leaves stripped

150g mayonnaise

Preheat the oven to 180°C/gas mark 4.

Heat a touch of the oil in a non-stick pan and add the limes, cut side down. Cook over a medium-high heat until caramelized, then set aside.

Halve the parsnips lengthways; if very long, quarter them first. Coat the parsnips lightly with oil, then arrange them in a single layer on a baking tray and roast until they are tender, 10–12 minutes. Leave to cool.

Put the flour on a small plate. Put the eggs and milk in a small bowl, whisk together and set aside. Combine the polenta, Parmesan, chilli, peppercorns and a good pinch of salt on a plate, mix well and set aside.

Coat the parsnip slices in the flour, dip into the egg mixture, then transfer immediately to the polenta mix and coat all over. Set aside and continue until all the pieces of parsnip are coated.

Heat the rest of the oil in a shallow pan until hot. Add the coated parsnips, working in batches if required, and fry until deep golden all over.

Remove and drain on kitchen paper, then arrange on a platter and finish with a good sprinkling of salt and tarragon leaves. Serve with the limes and mayonnaise.

BAKERY 5

BREADS

BUTTERNUT SQUASH
WHOLEMEAL FLOUR
CINNAMON
YOGHURT

MAKES 1 X 900G LOAF

I like a hint of sweetness for our bread platters, to balance out the tastes and textures of the other offerings, so this recipe gets a workout. It is not sweet like a dessert; it is more of a savoury cake. Pumpkin is as good as squash here, but it really depends on what is available, so feel free to use them interchangeably. Try this spread with soft goat's cheese. Fabulous.

550g self-raising wholemeal flour
65g psyllium husk powder
1 teaspoon baking powder
1 teaspoon bicarbonate of soda
½ teaspoon ground nutmeg
2½ teaspoons ground cinnamon
2 teaspoons ground ginger
a pinch of ground cloves
1 teaspoon fine salt
500g unpeeled butternut squash or pumpkin, cooked and roughly squished, a few slices reserved for the topping
160ml grape molasses or honey
4 eggs
125ml vegetable oil
180g non-fat Greek yoghurt
125ml milk
zest and juice of 1 lemon
1 tablespoon pumpkin seeds

Preheat the oven to 180°C/gas mark 4 and line a 900g loaf tin with baking parchment.

In a large mixing bowl, stir together the flour, psyllium powder, baking powder, bicarbonate of soda, nutmeg, cinnamon, ginger, cloves and salt.

Add the squash (or pumpkin), the molasses or honey, eggs, oil, yoghurt, milk and the lemon zest and juice. With a large rubber spatula, mix and fold until blended.

Transfer to the prepared tin and blob on the reserved squash (or pumpkin) slices on top, then sprinkle over the pumpkin seeds. Bake until deep golden brown on top, about 1 hour.

Remove from the oven, leave to cool for 5 minutes, then turn out on to a wire rack.

BACON
CHILLI
TOMATO
ROSEMARY
BEER

MAKES 4

A nifty little trick for utilizing the many empty tins I have lying around is to use them as serving containers. This super-simple recipe brings together some great flavours in an attractive presentation and is a good bit of fun.

2 tablespoons vegetable oil, plus extra for greasing

1 small red onion, halved and thinly sliced

4 rashers of bacon, trimmed and cut into matchsticks

½ a fresh red chilli, deseeded and thinly sliced

60g tinned chopped tomatoes

400g self-raising flour, plus extra for dusting

1 small sprig of fresh rosemary, leaves stripped and chopped

½ teaspoon fine salt

280ml beer, at room temperature

Grease and line the base only of four empty 400g tomato tins.

Put 1 tablespoon of the oil into a frying pan, add the onion and cook over a medium heat until soft. Add the bacon, chilli and tomatoes and cook for 2 minutes more, then set aside.

In a large bowl, combine the flour, rosemary and salt. Stir in the remaining 1 tablespoon of oil and the beer and mix until you have a sticky dough.

Turn on to a lightly floured work surface and roll out to a 20 x 35cm rectangle. Spread the dough with the onion mixture, then roll up lengthways to enclose the filling. Cut into four equal pieces and put them into the prepared tins, with the swirly bit facing up. Leave to stand for 30 minutes.

Preheat the oven to 180°C/gas mark 4.

Set the tins on a baking tray and bake until browned on top, about 40 minutes. Leave to cool, and serve in the tins.

POTATO
ROSEMARY

This is almost the only 'true' yeasted bread we make – it is so pretty as well as delicious that it is well worth the extra time needed for rising. But don't let this extra time put you off – it is still super easy to make and the presentation is impressive.

600g plain flour
1 tablespoon active dried yeast
2 teaspoons fine sea salt
2 teaspoons finely chopped fresh rosemary leaves
310ml warm water
5 tablespoons olive oil
2 potatoes, scrubbed
2 teaspoons sea salt flakes
12 sprigs of fresh rosemary
a handful of grated Parmesan cheese

In a large bowl, combine the flour, yeast, fine sea salt and rosemary and mix well. In a jug, combine the water and 3 tablespoons of the oil.

Make a well in the middle of the dry ingredients and pour in the water and oil mixture, stirring with your hands to bring it all together.

Transfer to a clean work surface and knead vigorously for at least 10 minutes, or until smooth and elastic. Return the dough to the bowl, cover with cling film or a tea towel and leave to rise for 45 minutes in a dry, warm place.

Slice the potatoes very thinly into rounds; a mandoline is ideal for this. Set aside half the slices for the topping. Punch the dough down, put back on the clean work surface and knead in the sliced potato for 2 minutes. Transfer to a 15 x 27cm non-stick loaf tin and set aside.

Coat the sliced potato for the topping with the remaining oil (toss in a bowl or use a brush) and stud the surface of the bread with the slices. Sprinkle over the sea salt flakes, scatter over the rosemary sprigs and the grated Parmesan and cover with a clean tea towel. Set aside to rise again, about 25 minutes.

Preheat the oven to 220°C/gas mark 7.

Bake the loaf until it is a deep golden brown, 35–45 minutes. Remove from the oven and leave to cool in the tin for 5 minutes, then turn out on to a wire rack.

chriskitch breads

Unlike loaves made with yeast, the breads we make at Chriskitch, with a few exceptions, are really savoury cakes. I simply do not have time for rising and kneading. But this doesn't mean I can't offer freshly baked bread, so the same goes for you. The bonus is that we are all absolved from kneading. What I do for most of these breads is closer to vigorous stirring, and the whole process is very forgiving. If you have a few specks of flour, don't worry; better to leave them, because if you over-knead it the bread will come out tough. Once you get going, the urge to experiment will surely kick in, so mess around and see what you get. Mix different flours, and add oats, seeds, nuts, dried fruit or different flakes, such as quinoa. Herbs, spices and cheeses can all be tinkered with. Go on, create your own.

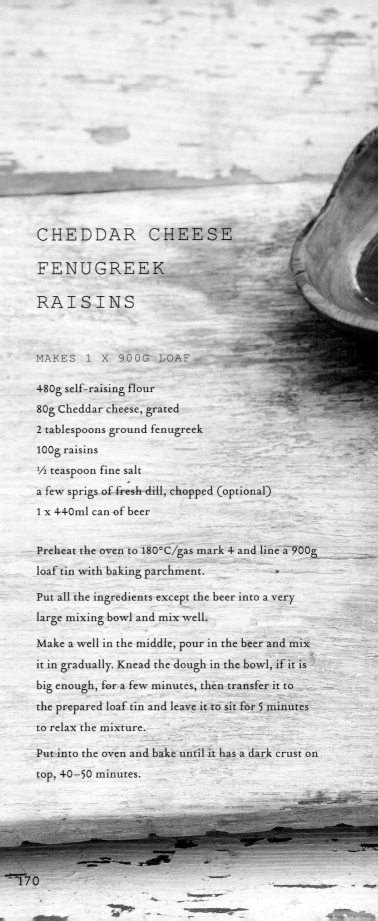

CHEDDAR CHEESE FENUGREEK RAISINS

MAKES 1 X 900G LOAF

480g self-raising flour
80g Cheddar cheese, grated
2 tablespoons ground fenugreek
100g raisins
½ teaspoon fine salt
a few sprigs of fresh dill, chopped (optional)
1 x 440ml can of beer

Preheat the oven to 180°C/gas mark 4 and line a 900g loaf tin with baking parchment.

Put all the ingredients except the beer into a very large mixing bowl and mix well.

Make a well in the middle, pour in the beer and mix it in gradually. Knead the dough in the bowl, if it is big enough, for a few minutes, then transfer it to the prepared loaf tin and leave it to sit for 5 minutes to relax the mixture.

Put into the oven and bake until it has a dark crust on top, 40–50 minutes.

CORNMEAL CHILLI PEPPERS RED ONION CHEDDAR CHEESE

SERVES 4-6

A modernized classic, really basic and best served straight from a cast-iron pan. Just remember that this material conducts heat well, so remove it from the oven the minute the edges go brown, as it will carry on cooking from the residual heat. An ordinary loaf tin works just fine too. This is perfect for playing around with.

500g cornmeal
2 pinches of granulated sugar
a pinch of salt
a pinch of freshly ground black pepper
10g garlic granules
½ teaspoon chilli flakes
2 teaspoons baking powder
1 teaspoon bicarbonate of soda
250ml milk
125g feta cheese, crumbled
100g Cheddar cheese, grated
180g tinned sweetcorn, drained
1 red pepper, deseeded and sliced
1 red onion, halved and sliced
a good handful of nigella seeds, to garnish
a few sprigs of fresh thyme

Preheat the oven to 180°C/gas mark 4. Line a 20cm cast-iron frying pan or 900g loaf tin with baking parchment.

In a large bowl, combine all the dry ingredients, apart from the nigella seeds, and stir to blend. Add the milk, cheese and corn and stir well, about 2 minutes.

Pour into the prepared pan or loaf tin, arrange the onion and red pepper slices on top and sprinkle over the nigella seeds and thyme. Bake until a skewer inserted in the middle comes out clean, 20–30 minutes.

ONION GARLIC

The only raising agent here is the flour, so this is about as basic as you get, bread-wise. I suppose it's like an Australian bushman's bread – flour, water, salt and not much more. Except there is a bit more; there is onion and garlic.

MAKES 1 X 900G LOAF

400g self-raising flour
1 large red onion, roughly chopped
2 garlic cloves, finely chopped
a pinch of sugar
½ teaspoon salt
65ml milk
250ml water

Preheat the oven to 180°C/gas mark 4.

Mix all the ingredients together in a large bowl. Knead lightly (about ten kneads) in the bowl, then transfer to a work surface and shape into a roll about 30cm long. With a sharp knife, make many diagonal scores close together across the top of the dough, then transfer to a baking tray and bake for 35–45 minutes until the bread sounds hollowed when tapped on the bottom.

BLUE CHEESE GUINNESS SUNFLOWER SEEDS

Is this even cooking? – I'm not really sure. Just throw it all into a bowl, mix, then bake. The only thing you need to know is that it will look cooked outside before it is done all the way through, so do the skewer thing. If you're really not sure, this can take a bit of overbaking, no problem.

MAKES 1 X 900G LOAF

400g self-raising flour
120g blue cheese
400ml Guinness
60g sunflower seeds, plus an extra handful
  for the topping
a pinch each of salt and sugar
a handful of pumpkin seeds
sea salt flakes, for the topping

Preheat the oven to 160°C/gas mark 3. Line a 900g loaf tin with baking parchment, leaving a generous overhang for lifting it out.

Put all the ingredients into a large mixing bowl and stir well to combine. Transfer to the prepared tin, scatter with sunflower seeds, pumpkin seeds and sea salt flakes, then bake for 50–60 minutes until a skewer inserted into the middle comes out dry.

Cool in the tin about 10 minutes, then lift out on to a wire rack to cool before serving.

CAKES

Customers are always bringing me produce from their gardens and allotments, which is so wonderful. To me it's proof of the connection I have with everyone in the neighbourhood, and it's just as good as having customers praise the food. They bring me gifts. In the autumn, I receive a bounty of windfall fruit and this is the sort of thing I might make with them – a large, dark spicy cake generously studded with apples and raisins. If you are lucky enough to have a strong-flavoured honey, use it here.

HONEY APPLE ALMOND CINNAMON

275g plain wholemeal flour
75g self-raising flour
2 teaspoons baking powder
3 tablespoons ground almonds
½ teaspoon ground cinnamon
½ teaspoon ground ginger
¼ teaspoon ground cloves
a good pinch of grated nutmeg
225g unsalted butter, softened
200g soft dark brown sugar
5 eggs
4 tablespoons full-flavoured honey
600g tart apples, peeled, cored and coarsely chopped
50g raisins
4 tablespoons milk
2–3 tablespoons flaked almonds
icing sugar, for dusting
Greek yoghurt or thick cream, for serving

Preheat the oven to 170°C/gas mark 3½ and line a 22cm springform cake tin with baking parchment.

In a mixing bowl, combine the flours, baking powder, ground almonds and spices and mix well. Set aside.

Using an electric hand mixer, beat together the butter and brown sugar in a mixing bowl until light and fluffy, at least 10 minutes. Add the eggs one at a time, beating well after each addition. Add the honey and mix until blended.

Add two-thirds of the flour mixture and beat on medium just until blended. Add the remaining flour mixture, fruit and milk and fold in with a spatula until just blended.

Transfer to the prepared tin, spread out evenly and sprinkle over the flaked almonds. Bake until brown on top, about 40 minutes, then cover loosely with foil and continue baking until a skewer inserted into the middle comes out clean – about 50–60 minutes more. Leave to cool in the tin for about 10 minutes, then release from the tin and dust the with icing sugar.

LEMON BASIL YOGHURT

SERVES 8

I suppose you could call this a virtuous cake. The richness and depth come from the yoghurt, so it tastes amazing without containing lashings of butter. There is no butter at all, in fact. This also keeps it light and allows the tartness of the lemon to shine through, while the basil adds just the right amount of peppery freshness.

3 eggs

250g caster sugar

zest and juice of 2 lemons

1 sprig of fresh basil, leaves roughly torn, plus a few sprigs to decorate

300g self-raising flour

280g Greek-style yoghurt

125ml vegetable oil

FOR THE LEMON SYRUP

2 lemons, zest peeled into fine strips

110g caster sugar

80ml fresh lemon juice

Preheat the oven to 180°C/gas mark 4. Grease a 24cm bundt tin, and line the base and sides with baking parchment. Alternatively, you can use a decorative silicone mould.

Using an electric mixer, beat the eggs and sugar until light and fluffy, for at least 10 minutes. Add the lemon zest and juice and the basil and beat just enough to incorporate.

Fold in the flour, yoghurt and oil until smooth. Spoon into the prepared tin and bake for 45 minutes, or until a skewer inserted into the middle comes out clean.

Meanwhile, make the lemon syrup. Put the lemon zest into a pan of boiling water for 1 minute, then drain and set aside. In the same pan, combine the sugar, lemon juice and 2 tablespoons of water and cook over a low heat, stirring, until the sugar dissolves. Simmer for 5 minutes, then add back the lemon zest.

While the cake is still in the tin, poke holes all over it using a skewer. Pour over half the hot syrup, allowing it to sink in before adding more. Leave to stand for 30 minutes before turning out.

Put on a serving plate and drizzle with the remaining syrup. Decorate with a few basil sprigs and serve.

GUINNESS DATES CHOCOLATE

With a very small restaurant, and a loyal local clientele, good staff is as important as good food and I have been incredibly lucky. Emily has been with us since very early on. Not only is she excellent at front of house, she bakes as well, and this is her recipe. In fact, in the beginning, she would bake this one for the cake table.

SERVES 8-10

1 x 235ml can of Guinness
250g unsalted butter, plus extra for greasing
90g cocoa powder
350g caster sugar
90ml milk
1 teaspoon vanilla extract
2 eggs
2 teaspoons bicarbonate of soda
1 teaspoon baking powder
300g plain flour
90g dried dates, pitted and very finely chopped

FOR THE ICING
100g white chocolate, finely chopped
200g cream cheese

Preheat the oven to 180°C/gas mark 4, and grease and line a 22cm springform cake tin.

In a large pan, combine the Guinness and butter and melt over a low heat. Remove from the heat, add the cocoa powder and sugar and stir to blend. Stir in the milk and vanilla, then add the eggs one at a time, mixing after each addition.

Put the bicarbonate of soda, baking powder and flour into a mixing bowl and stir to combine. Tip in the cocoa mixture, folding gently with a large spatula to blend thoroughly. Add the dates, give a quick mix, transfer to the prepared pan and bake until a skewer inserted in the middle comes out dry – about 40–50 minutes. Release from the tin and leave to cool on a wire rack.

Meanwhile, make the icing. Melt the white chocolate in a heatproof bowl over a pan of barely simmering water.
In a small bowl, stir together the melted chocolate and cream cheese and spread over the cooled cake.

CHOCOLATE
BUTTER
SUGAR
EGG
ALMOND

Equal quantities of ingredients is a standard formula for cake baking, and generally it is the weight of the eggs that determines the weight of the other ingredients. A fine dusting of cocoa powder on top adds an extra chocolatey hit and helps hide any imperfections, but wait until it cools, otherwise the powder melts to an unattractive sludge.

300g dark chocolate (70%), chopped
300g unsalted butter, in pieces
300g caster sugar
300g eggs (about 7–8)
30g ground almonds
a pinch of fine sea salt
a few tablespoons of cocoa powder, for dusting

Preheat the oven to 180°C/gas mark 4. Line a 22cm round cake tin with baking parchment.

Combine the chocolate and butter in a heatproof bowl set over a pan of boiling water. Stir often until almost completely melted, then remove the bowl from the heat and stir to finish melting. Add the sugar, stir to blend and set aside.

In another bowl, beat the eggs vigorously until completely combined. Add to the chocolate mixture along with the almonds and salt and fold in just enough to combine.

Transfer to the prepared tin and put into the oven. Lower the temperature to 150°C/gas mark 2 and bake for 20-30 minutes until the top of the cake cracks and is firm to the touch in the middle.

Leave to cool in the tin for 10 minutes before turning out on to a wire rack. Once the cake has cooled completely, put the cocoa powder into a sieve and dust the top of the cake with it.

BANANA
BROWN SUGAR

Australians do banana bread amazingly well, so this has to be a staple at any restaurant of mine. I suppose calling it a bread makes it less naughty to eat in large portions, but since we dress it up with a caramel topping and a mound of sugar-coated bananas I'm not sure it qualifies for bread status any more.

MAKES 1 X 900G LOAF

250g unsalted butter
180g demerara sugar
4 ripe or overripe bananas
260g plain flour
1 tablespoon bicarbonate of soda
1 tablespoon baking powder
2 eggs
120ml milk

FOR THE CARAMEL TOPPING
120g caster sugar
120ml double cream, at room temperature
2 firm, just-ripe bananas
icing sugar, for dusting

Preheat the oven to 180°C/gas mark 4 and line a 900g loaf tin with baking parchment.

In a pan, melt the butter over a low heat. Add the sugar and cook, stirring constantly, until it is almost dissolved – but it doesn't have to dissolve completely.

Add the bananas and blitz with a stick blender until combined; this does not have to be smooth, just blended. Alternatively, use a fork or a potato masher.

Put the flour, bicarbonate of soda and baking powder into a separate bowl and stir well to distribute everything evenly. Add the eggs one at a time, mixing after each addition. Stir in the milk. Add the banana mixture and stir to incorporate.

Scrape the mixture into the prepared loaf tin and bake until golden brown and a bit cracked on the top, about 45–60 minutes. Place the tin on a wire rack and bring to room temperature.

For the caramel topping, put the sugar into a small heavy-bottomed pan over a low heat. Cook, without stirring, until the sugar dissolves and begins to turn golden. Turn off the heat and carefully stir in about 1 tablespoon of the cream – the mixture will bubble a bit but then will settle. Repeat twice, then add the remaining cream and stir to blend. If you have any lumps, you can return it to a very low heat and stir constantly until dissolved.

Set the cake on a serving platter; it must be cooled off, otherwise the caramel won't set properly. Pour over the caramel evenly.

Slice the banana into long, thin lengthways strips and mound on top. Dust well with icing sugar to keep the bananas from browning, and serve.

ORANGE SEMOLINA ALMOND

SERVES 8–10

This is one of those traditional recipes I cannot really improve on or change in terms of ingredients. But adding a few randomly arranged orange slices to the bottom of the pan transforms this from ordinary cake to work of art. Also, adding a perfumed, brightly coloured cordial to the syrup brings it bang up to date.

3 lemons
2 oranges
350g fine semolina
2 teaspoons baking powder
200g ground almonds
250g unsalted butter, softened
450g caster sugar
1 teaspoon vanilla extract
5 eggs
1–2 teaspoons raspberry cordial (or use grenadine)

Preheat the oven to 170°C/gas mark 3½ and line a 22cm springform cake tin with baking parchment.

Grate the zest of 2 of the lemons and 1 orange. Trim away and discard the pith from the orange, then thinly slice. Place the orange slices in the base of the tin.

Put the semolina, baking powder and almonds into a bowl, mix well and set aside.

Using an electric hand whisk, beat together the butter, 250g of the sugar and the vanilla until light and lemon-coloured. Depending on the speed of your mixer this can take a while; for a really light, fluffy cake, be sure to beat very well at this stage.

Add the citrus zest and the eggs, one at a time, beating well after each addition.

Using a spatula, fold in the semolina and almond mixture until thoroughly blended. Pour into the tin on top of the orange slices and bake for about 1 hour, or until a skewer inserted into the middle comes out clean.

Meanwhile, prepare the syrup. Zest and juice the remaining lemon and orange. Put the remaining sugar into a pan with the juice, zest and cordial (or grenadine) and cook over a low heat until the sugar dissolves, stirring occasionally. Continue to cook until reduced by about half, then set aside.

When the cake is ready, remove from the oven and pierce it all over with a skewer while still in the tin. Pour two-thirds of the hot syrup over the hot cake and leave to stand for 15 minutes before releasing and inverting it on to a serving plate. Drizzle over the remaining syrup. Serve at room temperature.

Vegetables are great in sweet baking. If you think sweet potato, courgette, pumpkin, it's not such a stretch to get to parsnips, especially as they are naturally sweet. Parsnips also have a fantastic creamy quality, which gives the batter a nice texture. This is a showstopper of a cake, and tasty too.

SERVES 8–10

235g butter, plus extra for greasing
330g demerara sugar
125ml maple syrup
4 large eggs
330g self-raising flour
3 teaspoons baking powder
3 teaspoons mixed spice
300g parsnips, peeled and grated
1 medium eating apple, peeled, cored and grated
75g pecans, roughly chopped
zest and juice of 1 small orange

FOR THE TOPPING
100g caster sugar
225ml water
3 parsnips, peeled and quartered
a handful of whole pecans
350g mascarpone
5–6 tablespoons maple syrup

PARSNIP APPLE PECAN MAPLE SYRUP

Preheat the oven to 160°C/gas mark 3. Grease three 20cm sandwich tins and line the bases with baking parchment.

Melt the butter, demerara sugar and maple syrup in a large pan over a gentle heat, then leave to cool slightly. Whisk the eggs into this mixture, then stir in the flour, baking powder and mixed spice, followed by the grated parsnips and apple, chopped pecans and orange zest and juice. Divide between the prepared tins, then bake for 25–30 minutes until the tops spring back when pressed lightly.

Cool the cakes slightly in the tins for 10 minutes before turning them out on to wire racks to cool completely.

Meanwhile, raise the oven temperature to 200°C/gas mark 6 and line a baking tray with baking parchment.

For the topping, put the sugar and the water into a large pan and heat until the sugar dissolves. Add the quartered parsnips and cook just enough to soften them, about 5–7 minutes. Lift the parsnips out, reserving the sugar syrup, and transfer to the prepared baking tray, then bake until they turn an even golden brown. Remove and leave to cool.

Just before serving, mix together the mascarpone and maple syrup. Spread one-third of this mixture over one of the cakes and place another cake on top. Repeat, then spread the remaining mascarpone over the final cake layer. Pile the candied parsnips on top, scatter whole pecans over and drizzle over some of the remaining sugar syrup. Serve.

MIXED BERRIES
ROSE WATER
PISTACHIO

SERVES 8

Perfect for the timid baker,
this is an uncooked cake that
I like to call an 'icebox' cake.
Basically it sets in the fridge,
so there is no stress about
soggy bottoms or other pastry
dilemmas. It is super easy to
throw together, and thanks to all
the berries it is guaranteed to
be beautiful.

600g mixed berries, such as blackberries, raspberries,
  strawberries, blueberries
500ml double cream
1 teaspoon rose water, or to taste
125g caster sugar
400g plain biscuits, such as Nice, Rich Tea or butter
  biscuits
180g pistachios, toasted and roughly chopped
4 tablespoons pomegranate molasses

Set aside 100g of the whole berries for decoration, and slice
the rest. Put the sliced berries into a bowl and set aside.

Put the cream, rose water and sugar into a large mixing
bowl. Using an electric hand whisk, whip on high speed
just until the cream holds stiff peaks.

Line the base of a 22cm springform cake tin with some of
the biscuits – you may need to break them up and squish
them a bit to fit, otherwise leave them whole.

Spread a quarter of the cream on top of the biscuit
base. Top with a third of the sliced berries and chopped
pistachios, then add a drizzle of pomegranate molasses.
Repeat three more times, finishing with a layer of cream
and a drizzle of pomegranate molasses. Cover with cling
film and chill in the fridge for at least 4–6 hours.

When ready to serve, transfer to a serving plate, arrange
the reserved berries on top and serve chilled.

Note: The strength of rose water varies enormously, so
taste yours and adjust as needed. If there is too much, it
imparts an unpleasant 'soapy' taste.

This is a wheat-free cake, loaded with seed, nuts and spices. I especially like it with peaches, but you can use other stoned fruit: plums and nectarines are good, on their own or even combined.

PEACH CINNAMON QUINOA SEEDS

SERVES 8-10

80g unsalted butter

60g agave syrup

1 teaspoon ground nutmeg

1 teaspoon ground ginger

1 teaspoon ground cinnamon

6 fresh peaches (unpeeled), stoned and halved

FOR THE SEED BASE

30g unsalted butter

2 tablespoons agave syrup

2 tablespoons barley flakes

85g uncooked red quinoa

2 tablespoons ground almonds

2 tablespoons sunflower seeds

2 tablespoons pumpkin seeds

2 tablespoons linseeds

a handful of pecans, coarsely chopped

Preheat the oven to 180°C/gas mark 4 and line a 22cm springform cake tin with baking parchment.

In a large non-stick frying pan, combine the butter, agave syrup and spices and cook over a medium heat until melted. Add the peaches and cook gently for 15 minutes.

For the seed base, combine the butter and agave syrup in a small saucepan and melt over a low heat.

In a mixing bowl, combine the remaining ingredients, then pour over the melted butter mixture. Stir well to blend.

Arrange the cooked peaches in the lined dish, cut side down in a single layer. Top with the seed mixture and pack down firmly.

Bake for 45–60 minutes, then remove and allow to cool for 15 minutes in the tin. Release from the tin and invert on to a serving plate and serve at room temperature.

Many of our customers appreciate
vegan and gluten-free options
on the cake table, and this one
satisfies both. It is so good
that even those without dietary
concerns love it. You will need
to chill the coconut milk 24 hours
in advance.

SERVES 8-10

ALMOND
COCOA POWDER
MAPLE SYRUP
AVOCADO

375g almond flour

35g cocoa powder

2 teaspoons baking powder

1 teaspoon ground cinnamon

2 tablespoons maple syrup

1 teaspoon vanilla extract

1 overripe banana, squished with a fork

60g coconut oil

4 tablespoons cider vinegar

FOR THE ICING

1 x 375ml tin of coconut milk, refrigerated for at least
24 hours

2 ripe avocados, peeled and stoned

35g cocoa powder

2 tablespoons honey, plus extra for drizzing

4 tablespoons coconut oil, melted

1 teaspoon vanilla extract

Preheat the oven to 180°C/gas mark 4 and line a
22cm springform cake tin with baking parchment.

Combine the dry ingredients and set aside.

In a large bowl, combine the maple syrup,
vanilla extract and banana. Set aside.

Melt the coconut oil in a small saucepan over a
very low heat. Add to the banana mixture, along
with the dry ingredients and vinegar, and stir
well to blend.

Pour into the prepared tin and bake for about
30 minutes, or until a skewer inserted into the
middle comes out clean.

Allow to cool fully, as the cake may crumble
otherwise, then transfer to a cake plate.

For the icing, put all the ingredients into a food
processor and whiz to blend. Transfer to a shallow
baking dish and smooth out to an even layer, then
refrigerate until set.

To decorate, use a soup spoon to scoop out scrolls
of the icing and arrange, haphazardly, on top of
the cake. Serve in wedges, with some extra honey
drizzled over.

BUTTER
EGG
VANILLA
MIXED BERRIES

MAKES 8

260g self-raising flour
200g caster sugar
80ml milk
80g unsalted butter, melted
2 eggs, beaten
1 teaspoon vanilla extract
200g mixed berries, fresh or frozen
icing sugar, for dusting (optional)

Preheat the oven to 200°C/gas mark 6 and line a muffin tray with paper cases.

Mix the flour and sugar together in a mixing bowl. Add the milk and melted butter and fold together lightly once or twice with a spatula; do not combine completely.

Add the eggs and fold a few times more, then add the berries and do the final folding, gently, to blend completely. A few lumps of flour are fine; the important thing is not to overmix.

Divide the mixture equally between the muffin cases, filling them almost to the top.

Bake for 15–25 minutes until puffed and golden, then remove from the oven and leave to cool. Dust with icing sugar when completely cool if desired.

Two of our muffin recipes. One is our basic batter to which we add whatever bits are to hand on the day: apple, pear, chocolate, dried fruit, but berries are definitely the prettiest. The other is vegan and nicely spiced. These are best eaten fresh from the oven, and the yields are smallish.

APPLE
QUINOA
MACADAMIA NUT
SOYA MILK

MAKES 8

2 apples, peeled, cored and cut into 1cm chunks

60g olive oil-based spread, melted

1 teaspoon vanilla essence

125ml soya milk

130g self-raising flour

185g cooked quinoa (about 60g uncooked)

1 teaspoon baking powder

½ teaspoon fine sea salt

200g caster sugar

2 teaspoons ground cinnamon

1 teaspoon grated nutmeg

1 teaspoon ground allspice

100g macadamia nuts, coarsely chopped

icing sugar, for dusting (optional)

Preheat the oven to 180°C/gas mark 4 and line a muffin tray with paper cases.

Put half the apples into a saucepan and add a splash of water. Cook over a low heat, stirring, until soft and squishy. Do not dilute the apples but do add a little more water if necessary to keep the mixture from burning before the apples are cooked. When tender, mash roughly with a wooden spoon, transfer to a large mixing bowl and set aside.

When the apples are cool-ish, stir in the melted spread, vanilla and soya milk and mix well. Set aside.

In another bowl, combine the flour, quinoa, baking powder, salt, sugar and spices. Fold half of this into the apple mixture until just blended, then add the rest, along with the remaining apple chunks and the nuts, and stir just enough to blend.

Spoon the mixture equally between the muffin cases, filling them almost to the top.

Bake for 15–25 minutes until puffed and golden, then remove from the oven and leave to cool. Dust with icing sugar when completely cool if desired.

BISCUIT
CREAM CHEESE
TONKA BEAN

MAKES 4 MINI CAKES

300g plain biscuits, such as Hobnobs

75g unsalted butter, melted

500g cream cheese

50g caster sugar

½ a tonka bean

3 eggs

a pinch of fine sea salt

There is nothing particularly revolutionary about cheesecake but it is a solid favourite, which is useful if you are running a restaurant. The jars make it even more attractive, and easy on so many levels: they are at once baking dish, serving plate and storage container. To make mine just that little bit different I like to add a grating of tonka bean. Simple, pretty, yummy. Hard to do better than that.

You will need 4 mini 150ml preserving jars, rubber rims removed for baking.

Put the biscuits into a bowl and bash into crumbs. I use the bottom of a rolling pin. Stir in the melted butter.

Divide the crumb mixture between the jars, pressing it into the bottom in an even layer. Refrigerate to set – at least 15 minutes.

Preheat the oven to 140°C/gas mark 1.

Combine the cream cheese and sugar in a mixing bowl and beat to blend and lighten. Grate in the tonka bean. Add the eggs one at a time, mixing well after each addition, then add the salt.

Set the jars on a baking tray and divide the cream cheese mixture between them, pouring it in to fill almost to the top.

Transfer the tray to the oven and bake until the cheesecakes are golden and cracked on the top, 20–35 minutes. Remove and leave to cool, then refrigerate to chill completely. Serve in the jars.

Note: This can also be made in individual mini springform tins.

PRUNE
PEAR
CROISSANT
CHOCOLATE

8 baby pears

250ml milk

250ml double cream

4 eggs

75g caster sugar

1 teaspoon vanilla extract

6 mini croissants, thickly sliced

100g dark chocolate, chopped bar or chips

100g pitted prunes (about 4 or 5)

icing sugar, for dusting

SERVES 4–6

What to do with stale croissants can be a problem, but this is what we do with ours at Chriskitch. It is nothing more than a version of bread and butter pudding, so you could easily replace the croissants with something else – whatever you have to hand that is slightly stale will probably be fine. However, adding fresh and dried fruit turns it into something more substantial, and I am particularly fond of combining pears, prunes and chocolate. Make this and you will see why.

Preheat the oven to 160°C/gas mark 3 and line a 30cm x 18cm (brownie) tray with baking parchment.

Cut each pear in half lengthways and set aside.

In a large mixing bowl, whisk together the milk, cream, eggs, sugar and vanilla until just blended. Arrange the croissant slices in the pan and put the pear halves in between. Pour over the cream mixture. Scatter the chocolate and prunes all around.

Bake until puffed and golden, 25–30 minutes. Leave to cool, then dust with icing sugar and cut into portions to serve.

EXTRAS 6

DRINKS

WATER
FENNEL
CUCUMBER
MINT

MAKES 1 LITRE

1 litre water
1 slice of fennel bulb, with fronds
a few long thin slices of cucumber
a few leaves of fresh mint

Combine all the ingredients in a jug and
refrigerate for a few hours before serving.

WATER
LEMON
THYME

MAKES 1 LITRE

1 litre water
juice of 1 lemon
a few sprigs of fresh thyme

Combine all the ingredients in a jug, mix
well and refrigerate overnight.

PEACH
TARRAGON
CHILLI

2 ripe peaches, stoned and quartered
75g caster sugar
juice of 1 lemon
2–3 sprigs of fresh tarragon
1 fresh red chilli, deseeded and sliced
1 litre water
a few drops of peach flavouring, (optional)

Combine all the ingredients in a jug, mix well and refrigerate overnight.

Serve in glasses, with extra peach slices for garnish if desired.

LEMON
SUGAR

MAKES 1 LITRE

juice of 3 lemons
125g caster sugar
1 litre sparkling water
a few fresh lemon slices

In a small pan, combine the lemon juice and sugar over a low heat and cook until just dissolved. Leave to cool, then add the water and refrigerate for at least a few hours. Serve with fresh lemon slices.

GINGER
LEMON

MAKES JUST OVER 2 LITRES

125g fresh ginger, peeled
200g caster sugar
1½ tablespoons lemon juice
¼ teaspoon active dried yeast
a pinch of fine sea salt
2 litres water

Using a microplane grater, grate enough ginger to obtain 3½ tablespoons. Put the grated ginger into a sieve set over a bowl and press down to extract the juice. Discard the ginger solids.

In a jug, combine the ginger juice, sugar, lemon juice, yeast and fine salt. Add the water and stir to dissolve the sugar.

Leave to stand at room temperature for 2–3 hours to ferment, then refrigerate for at least 24 hours before serving. Due to fermentation, do not seal the container; just cover it lightly with a cloth. Store in the refrigerator and use within 1 week.

BERRIES
WATER

MAKES 1 LITRE

1 litre water
a few fresh berries, whatever is to hand
3–4 tablespoons (or to taste) blackcurrant or
    strawberry cordial, or grenadine

Combine all the ingredients in a jug, mix well and refrigerate overnight.

tea service

Tea at Chriskitch is not just a bag in a mug,
though we do that as well. The idea of our tea
service is to allow customers to play with
flavourings, so we offer a range of bits and
pieces to add to the tea, or just to hot water.

Ingredients are usually all of the following:
chrysanthemum flowers, honey, lemongrass, fresh
orange and lemon, fresh mint, cinnamon stick,
fresh ginger, large green cardamom pods,
fenugreek seeds, tea bag.

A few traditional infusion combos would be:
Indian chai (fenugreek, cinnamon, cardamom),
Thai (ginger and lemongrass) or simply whatever
– chrysanthemum and citrus; mint, honey and
lemon; just cinnamon.

SALAD DRESSINGS

The general formula for my dressings is 1-2-3. Part 1 is acid, part 2 is flavour, part 3 is oil.

The choice of oil depends on the other ingredients; use a very good olive oil for dressings, or a neutral vegetable oil if the other flavours are powerful. You can also mix oils, half olive/ half vegetable, and even throw in some other flavours like pumpkin seed oil, hazelnut oil or palm heart oil. These tend to be quite powerful, though, so use them in small doses.

The important thing is to be forthright with your seasoning. A tiny bit of dressing coats a hefty portion of salad, so be bold and go big.

You can prepare your dressing right before using, but most taste best the next day.

HERB DRESSING
Take 50g mixed fresh herbs (parsley, coriander, chives, whatever), 50ml wine vinegar, 1 teaspoon fine salt, a good grinding of black pepper and 150ml extra virgin olive oil. Put into a screwtop jar and shake well. Taste and adjust the seasoning. Goes with everything.

HONEY AND MUSTARD DRESSING
Take 50ml wine vinegar, 4 tablespoons wholegrain Dijon mustard, 50ml honey, 1 teaspoon fine salt, a good grinding of black pepper and 150ml vegetable oil. Put into a screwtop jar and shake well. Taste and adjust the seasoning. Good with potatoes and cauliflower as a marinade.

LEMON DRESSING
Boil 2 lemons twice: boil once for 30 minutes, drain, then add fresh water and boil again for 30 minutes. In a food processor, blitz up the boiled lemons with 100ml wine vinegar, 1 teaspoon fine salt, a good grinding of black pepper and 250ml vegetable oil. Put into a screwtop jar and shake well. Taste and adjust the seasoning. Use for poached fish, green bean salad or an iceberg lettuce and crouton salad.

CHAMOMILE DRESSING
Take 50ml malt vinegar, 1 teaspoon vanilla extract, the contents of 1 chamomile tea bag, a drizzle of honey, 1 teaspoon fine salt, a good grinding of black pepper and 150ml extra virgin olive oil. Put into a screwtop jar and shake well. Taste and adjust the seasoning. Nice on scallops.

TAHINI DRESSING
Take 150g tahini, the juice of 2 lemons, a splash of white wine vinegar, a pinch of sea salt, a good grinding of black pepper and a drizzle of olive oil. Put into a screwtop jar and shake well. Taste and adjust the seasoning. Store in the fridge.

WATERMELON
CIDER VINEGAR
CLOVES

MAKES 2–3 JARS

1 watermelon, rind only

600g caster sugar

375ml cider vinegar

250ml malt vinegar

125ml balsamic vinegar

4 tablespoons mixed pickling spice

1 tablespoon whole black peppercorns

10 whole cloves

a small piece of fresh ginger, thinly sliced

3 cinnamon sticks, broken into pieces

2 teaspoons whole allspice

You will also need 2–3 large jars with vinegar-proof lids.

Wash the watermelon rind and cut away all the green parts – you only want the white. Cut into bite-sized pieces. Put the rind into a large pan and add cold water to cover. Bring to the boil over a high heat, then lower the heat and simmer until tender, 20–30 minutes. Drain and set aside.

Meanwhile, in another large stainless steel pan, combine the remaining ingredients and simmer gently for 15 minutes. Cover and set aside.

Put the rinds into sterilized jars to come almost to the top, and pour over the vinegar mixture, filling the jars right up. Store in the fridge – the rinds will keep for a few months.

Note: To sterilize jars, heat the oven to 140°C/gas mark 1. Wash the jars in hot, soapy water, then rinse well. Place the jars on a baking sheet and put them in the oven to dry completely. If using Kilner jars, boil the rubber seals, as dry heat damages them.

CHERRY
CIDER VINEGAR
CRANBERRY
APPLE

MAKES ABOUT 3 JARS

2 tablespoons extra virgin olive oil

2 onions, finely chopped

2 garlic cloves, finely chopped

65g soft brown sugar

350g frozen pitted cherries

1 teaspoon mixed spice

½ teaspoon ground ginger

375ml cider vinegar

200g dried cranberries

6 large apples, peeled, cored and chopped
   to cherry size

zest and juice of 1 orange

2 tablespoons brandy

5 cloves

1 cinnamon stick

2 star anise

You will also need 2–3 large jars with vinegar-proof lids.

Heat the oil in a large stainless steel pan over a medium heat. Add the onions and garlic and cook, stirring, until soft, about 3 minutes.

Add the sugar, cherries, mixed spice, ginger, vinegar, cranberries, apples, orange zest and juice, brandy, spices and 250ml water. Bring to the boil, then reduce the heat to low and simmer, stirring occasionally, for about 1 hour.

Leave to cool slightly, then spoon into sterilized jars (see *Note* opposite). Keep refrigerated and use within 1 week.

212

BLACK GRAPE
BALSAMIC
RED WINE

MAKES 2-3 JARS

1kg black grapes, seeds removed

100g soft brown sugar

80ml balsamic vinegar

80ml red wine

2 star anise

2 cloves

1 bay leaf

Put all the ingredients into a stainless steel pan and bring just to the boil, then lower the heat and simmer gently for about 20 minutes.

Leave to cool, then spoon into sterilized jars (see page 212) and refrigerate. It will keep for about 2–3 weeks.

CHERRY
BROWN SUGAR
SMOKED PAPRIKA

MAKES 2-3 JARS

200g frozen pitted cherries

60ml Worcestershire sauce

150g tomato ketchup

65g soft brown sugar

2 tablespoons maple syrup

2 tablespoons apple cider vinegar

1 tablespoon Dijon mustard

3 teaspoons smoked paprika

1 teaspoon dried oregano

1 teaspoon ground cumin

3 cloves

½ tablespoon instant coffee

Put all the ingredients into a stainless steel pan and cook over a low heat, stirring, for 2–3 minutes. Raise the heat a bit and cook until the sauce has thickened, about 5 minutes, then spoon into sterilized jars (see page 212) and refrigerate. It will keep for about 2–3 weeks.

BUTTERNUT SQUASH PRESERVED LEMON

MAKES 2–3 JARS

1 small butternut squash (about 1kg)
2 tablespoons extra virgin olive oil
1 red onion, finely sliced
1 teaspoon paprika
1 teaspoon ground cumin
½ teaspoon ground ginger
1 garlic clove, finely chopped
1 preserved lemon, rind only, finely sliced
juice of ½ a lemon
a good pinch of fine salt
a good pinch of freshly ground black pepper

Peel the squash and remove the seeds, then cut into small pieces.

Heat the oil in a frying pan, add the onion and cook until just soft, about 3 minutes. Add the spices and garlic and cook for 1 minute more.

Add the squash, preserved lemon, lemon juice and 2 tablespoons of water and simmer for about 15 minutes, or until the squash is just tender. Add a little more water if it looks like it's drying out too much. Season with salt and pepper.

Leave the relish to stand for at least 30 minutes before serving. It will keep in sterilized jars (see page 212) in the fridge for about 1 week, or it can be frozen.

COCONUT CORIANDER

MAKES 2–3 JARS

280g fresh coconut, grated or chopped
1 bunch of fresh coriander
juice of 1 lime
2 green Thai chillies, deseeded and pith removed
2½cm piece of fresh ginger, peeled and grated
¼ teaspoon fine salt

Put all the ingredients into a food processor and add 150ml of water. Process until smooth. Taste and adjust, adding more lime juice and salt as needed. If the mixture is too thick, thin it with a little more water.

Leave the chutney to stand for at least 30 minutes before serving. It will keep in sterilized jars (see page 212) in the fridge for about 1 week, or it can be frozen.

FLAVOURED
SALTS
AND
SUGARS

Keep a good selection of flavoured
salts and sugars around to widen
your culinary repertoire. Experiment
with single or mixed herbs and
spices: nigella and fennel seed
salt, cardamom and coffee sugar,
dried blueberries and sugar,
powdered wasabi and salt, amchur
(dried mango powder), dried
mulberries and salt, star anise and
sugar. You get the idea.

Shelf life is as for any spice
mix: store in a sealed container
away from light and humidity, but
fresh herbs and dried fruit tend to
shorten the lifespan.

SALTS

MANDARIN SALT

Spread the peel of 2 mandarins on a microwave-proof plate lined with kitchen paper, microwave on the lowest power (defrost or dehydrate) and cook until dehydrated. The time varies, so go slow and keep an eye. In a spice blender or coffee grinder, break up the dried peel, add 100g sea salt flakes and blitz until powdered.

SESAME SALT

In a small non-stick frying pan, toast 50g sesame seeds until golden brown. Transfer to a plate and leave to cool completely. In a spice blender or coffee grinder, break up the dried peel, add 100g Maldon sea salt and blitz until powdered. Make sure the seeds are completely cooled before you blitz them or you will get a paste rather than a dry mixture.

CHAMOMILE SALT

Put 20g dried chamomile flowers without stems and 100g Maldon sea salt into a spice blender or coffee grinder. Pulse until combined; the mixture should be coarse.

SUGARS

MINT OR BASIL SUGAR

In a small food processor, combine 40g fresh mint or basil leaves and 200g caster sugar. Blitz until smooth. This will lose its colour after 4–5 days.

PRESERVED LEMON SUGAR

Wash a preserved lemon well and pat dry. Trim away the flesh and use for another recipe. In a small food processor, mix the preserved lemon peel with 200g caster sugar and blitz until smooth.

CINNAMON SUGAR

Mix together 1 tablespoon ground cinnamon and 200g caster sugar in a small bowl until blended. Add a squidge more cinnamon to taste if desired.

WALNUTS
VINEGAR

MAKES 2–3 JARS

1kg green walnuts

2 teaspoons fine sea salt

1.5 litres malt vinegar

1 teaspoon black peppercorns

1 teaspoon ground allspice

1 knob of fresh ginger, thinly sliced

1 teaspoon grated horseradish

2 garlic cloves

2 bay leaves

You will also need 2–3 large jars with vinegar-proof lids

Wipe the walnuts clean with a cloth and prick the shells all over with a needle to allow the flavours to penetrate. Put them into a large stainless steel pan and add cold water to cover well. Bring to the boil, add 1 teaspoon of the salt and boil for 10 minutes.

Remove from the heat and let the walnuts cool in the brine. Refrigerate for 1 week, then repeat, starting with fresh salted water. The walnuts need a total of 2 weeks' soaking time.

After the 2 weeks, remove the walnuts from the brine. Spread them on a tray and leave them out to air-dry overnight; they will look black and awful – but that's fine.

In a large stainless steel pan, combine the vinegar, peppercorns, allspice, ginger, horseradish, garlic and bay leaves. Add the walnuts and bring to the boil, then reduce the heat and simmer for 10 minutes. Transfer everything to sterilized jars (see page 212) ensuring the liquid covers the walnuts. The walnuts will keep in the fridge for about 3 months.

VEGETABLES
VERJUICE

MAKES ABOUT 2 JARS

1kg baby carrots with green tops, scrubbed (or use green tomatoes or sliced red pepper)

375ml cups verjuice

125ml apple cider vinegar

150g caster sugar

1 tablespoon pink peppercorns

2 teaspoons coriander seeds

a few sprigs of fresh dill

garlic cloves (optional)

1 red onion, sliced (optional)

fine sea salt

You will also need 2 large jars with vinegar-proof lids

Trim the carrot tops, leaving about 1–2cm of stalk.

In a large bowl or jug, combine the remaining ingredients and stir to dissolve the sugar.

Bring a large pan of salted water to the boil and add the carrots. Cook for 2–3 minutes, to barely blanch them. Drain well.

Arrange the carrots (or tomatoes or peppers) in sterilized jars (see page 212) and pour over the verjuice mixture to fill. Make sure to get all the spices and herbs in the jars with the vegetables. Refrigerate for a few days before serving. The carrots will keep in the fridge for up to 1 month.

INDEX

ACKNOWLEDGEMENTS

Chris and Laura would like to thank everyone at Octopus Publishing for having faith in the project and for being so fantastic to work with, but especially Alison Starling, Juliette Norsworthy and Sybella Stephens. For making this book look so gorgeous, huge thanks to Tamin Jones, Stephanie Howard, Liz Belton and Miranda Harvey. If there is anyone we forgot to mention, thank you, and forgive us our lousy memories.

Chris

For being terrific and contributing so much to the success of Chriskitch and this book in particular, I would like to thank: Marcin Dolgij, Emily Ashton, Deborah Todd, Kylie Honor and Laura Washburn Hutton. Special thanks to my wonderful agent, Jonny Geller. And last but always first, my amazing partner, my rock and my pillar of strength, Bogusia and my two beautiful kids, Kayah and Oleana.

Laura

Chefs rarely allow their writing partners equal share on the front cover and for this, and for asking me to help with the book, thank you so much Christian Honor. Thank you Kate Morris for the occasional testing help, and thanks to the team at my house: Clara, Julian, Joseph and, of course, Ian.

ABOUT THE AUTHORS

Chris Honor has worked with a range of world-class chefs during his diverse career –
including Gordon Ramsay, David Nicolas, Chris Janson and Henry Brosi. He has worked
all over the world and managed a team of 120 chefs at The Dorchester in London, but
wanted to return to his cooking roots when launching his own restaurant. His new
venture, Chriskitch, based in Muswell Hill, north London and Shoreditch, east London
uses his Australian upbringing, classical French training and worldwide experiences to
create fantastically flavourful food that has customers queuing round the block.

Since graduating from the prestigious Ecole de Cuisine La Varenne in Paris, **Laura
Washburn Hutton** has had a number of careers. In Paris, she worked as an assistant
to Patricia Wells. Later, after moving to London, she worked as a commissioning
editor, overseeing the publication of many cookery books as well as writing numerous
publications herself. Opting for a better work-life balance, she has slowed down the pace
to be able to 'have the time to actually cook instead of only reading about it'. She now
combines writing about food with teaching people to cook.